watchOS With SwiftUI by Tutorials

By Scott Grosch

watchOS With SwiftUI by Tutorials

Scott Grosch

Notice of Rights

Notice of Liability

Trademarks

ISBN: 978-1-950325-84-9

Table of Contents

Book License

By purchasing *watchOS With SwiftUI by Tutorials*, you have the following license:

- You are allowed to use and/or modify the source code in *watchOS With SwiftUI by Tutorials* in as many apps as you want, with no attribution required.
- You are allowed to use and/or modify all art, images and designs that are included in *watchOS With SwiftUI by Tutorials* in as many apps as you want, but must include this attribution line somewhere inside your app: "Artwork/images/designs: from *watchOS With SwiftUI by Tutorials*, available at www.kodeco.com".
- The source code included in *watchOS With SwiftUI by Tutorials* is for your personal use only. You are NOT allowed to distribute or sell the source code in *watchOS With SwiftUI by Tutorials* without prior authorization.
- This book is for your personal use only. You are NOT allowed to reproduce or transmit any part of this book by any means, electronic or mechanical, including photocopying, recording, etc. without previous authorization. You may not sell digital versions of this book or distribute them to friends, coworkers or students without prior authorization. They need to purchase their own copies.

All materials provided with this book are provided on an "as is" basis, without warranty of any kind, express or implied, including but not limited to the warranties of merchantability, fitness for a particular purpose and noninfringement. In no event shall the authors or copyright holders be liable for any claim, damages or other liability, whether in an action of contract, tort or otherwise, arising from, out of or in connection with the software or the use or other dealings in the software.

All trademarks and registered trademarks appearing in this guide are the properties of their respective owners.

Before You Begin

This section tells you a few things you need to know before you get started, such as what you'll need for hardware and software, where to find the project files for this book, and more.

What You Need

To follow along with this book, you'll need the following:

- A Mac running macOS Ventura (13.0) or later.
- It is strongly recommended to have an Apple Watch with watchOS 9.0 or higher
- Xcode 14.3 or later. Xcode is the main development tool for iOS. You'll need Xcode 14.3 or later to make use of SwiftUI and the latest features explained throughout the book. You can download the latest version of Xcode from Apple's developer site here: apple.co/2asi58y — If you have an Apple Developer account, you can also download any Xcode version here: apple.co/3GWcz96.

> **Note**: The code covered in this book was developed and tested with Swift 5.8, macOS Ventura and Xcode 14.3 — so even though you can work with slightly earlier versions of them, we encourage you to update to those versions to follow along the book without unexpected errors.

Book Source Code & Forums

Where to Download the Materials for This Book

The materials for this book can be cloned or downloaded from the GitHub book materials repository:

- https://github.com/kodecocodes/wos-materials/tree/editions/2.0

Forums

We've also set up an official forum for the book at forums.kodeco.com/c/books/watchos-with-swiftui. This is a great place to ask questions about the book or to submit any errors you may find.

"This book is dedicated to my wife and daughter, both of whom gave up many a night so that I could work on it, as well as to my parents who always made sure a good education was a priority."

— Scott Grosch

About the Author

Scott Grosch has been involved with iOS app development since the first release of the public SDK from Apple. He mostly works with a small set of clients on a couple large apps. During the day, Scott is a Solutions Architect at a Fortune 500 company in the Pacific Northwest. At night, he's still working on figuring out how to be a good parent to a toddler with his wife.

About the Editors

Pablo Mateo is the final pass editor for this book. He is Delivery Manager at at one of the biggest Banks in the world, and was also founder and CTO of a Technology Development company in Madrid. His expertise is focused on web and mobile app development, although he first started as a Creative Art Director. He has been for many years the Main Professor of the iOS and Android Mobile Development Masters Degree at a well-known technology school in Madrid (CICE). He has a masters degree in Artificial Intelligence & Machine-Learning and is currently learning Quantum Computing at MIT.

Nick Rogness is a tech editor for this book. He has been writing code professionally since 2004 and an iOS developer since iOS 9. He looks for any reason to get outdoors, running, biking, hiking, camping, whatever it takes.

Piotr Fulmanski is a tech editor for this book. Piotr has been working at the Faculty of Mathematics and Computer Science of the University of Lodz since 2001 where he teaches various computer science subjects. When he is not preparing materials for his students, he runs in the forest or makes toys for his children. He spends his vacation in the mountains with his family.

Kirk Ericson is the English language editor for this book. He has worked for several daily and weekly newspapers as an editor, copy editor, reporter and columnist, and has worked several side jobs to ride out the bad times at newspapers. He lives in Olympia, Washington, and is a graduate of Western Washington University in Bellingham and Browne Elementary School in Spokane. Kirk has two children, a son and a son, and in his own time, he shoots free throws, and plays yoga and ping-pong.

Introduction

Since the Apple Watch came out in 2015, it has taken a dominant position in the market, becoming an indispensable tool for many users. It has proven to be a tremendously useful device that lets you see all your notifications without having to take out the phone and check valuable information from your favorite apps at a glance. It has even become the perfect companion for those who like participating in all kinds of sports.

This book will teach you how to make the most of the Apple Watch, showing you the powerful functionalities this small device provides for app developers. You'll learn how to show notifications, use snapshots to provide updated information, why complications are so important and even how to integrate HealthKit into your apps! And that's just the start of what you'll discover by reading this book.

Best of all, you'll do all this using **SwiftUI**, the declarative framework Apple designed for building apps. You'll see how easy it is to build incredible apps for your Watch.

We hope you enjoy this book almost as much as we've enjoyed creating it. We can't wait to see what you'll build after reading it!

How to read this book

You can read this book from cover to cover, but you can also pick and choose the chapters that interest you the most, or the chapters you need immediately for your current projects. Some chapters go together, like the ones about complications, but most can be read independently.

We also recommend that you read *SwiftUI Apprentice* or *SwiftUI by Tutorials* if you don't have a strong knowledge on the SwiftUI framework.

Finally, for all readers, Kodeco is committed to providing quality, up-to-date learning materials. We'd love to have your feedback. What parts of the book gave you one of those *aha* learning moments? Were any topics confusing? Did you spot a typo or an error? Let us know at forums.kodeco.com and look for the particular forum category for this book. We'll make an effort to take your comments into account in the book's next update.

Section I: watchOS With SwiftUI

Chapter 1: Hello, Apple Watch

By Scott Grosch

In 2015, Apple promised the world it was going to release a new, revolutionary device. On April 24, 2015, it released the first generation Apple Watch to the public. Some people felt the device was awesome and had huge potential, while others were firmly in the *"meh"* camp.

Full disclosure, I was initially one of the latter people.

However, with the addition of features like the Wallet and Apple Pay, as well as the option to purchase cellular data plans for the watch, it's hard to dismiss the device as a fad. Whatever your feelings regarding the Apple Watch, it's a part of the Apple ecosystem you'll definitely want to support to ensure maximum exposure for your apps.

During this chapter, you'll create your first watchOS app and see how much of your existing iOS development knowledge directly transfers to the Apple Watch.

Hello, World!

Open Xcode and create a new project by selecting **File ▸ New ▸ Project...** or pressing **Shift-Command-N**. In the dialog window where you choose your project type, select the **watchOS** tab and then choose the **App** template:

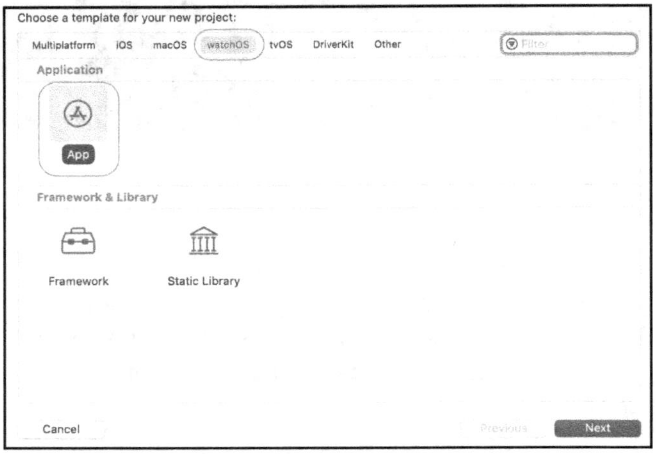

Press **Next** and, after selecting location for your project, you'll see the standard options dialog. Enter a **Product Name**, such as **HelloAppleWatch**, and be sure that **Watch-only App** is checked:

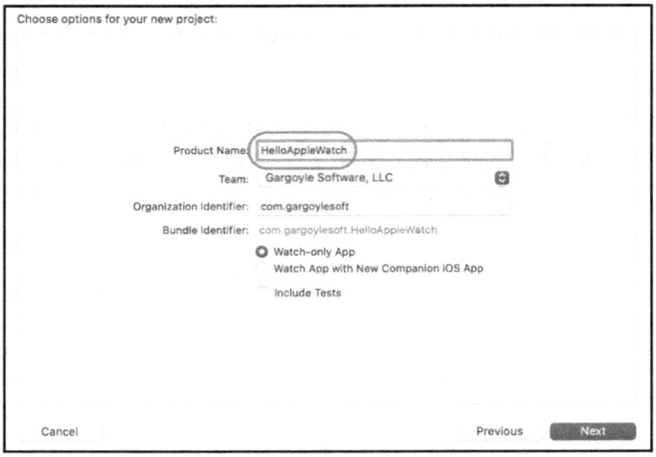

When developing projects that support the Apple Watch, you can choose whether you'll provide a companion iOS app. Since this book aims to teach items specific to watchOS development, most of the chapters focus exclusively on the watchOS project. Only features that require a companion iOS app will include an iOS project.

Select **Product ▸ Run** or press **Command-R** to build and run the app. After a moment, the Apple Watch simulator will appear and show a spinner:

It usually takes a few minutes for the simulator to load the watchOS app, so don't worry if the app doesn't start immediately. After a while, you'll see the obligatory "Hello, World!" example that all good programming books start with:

It's Just SwiftUI

Take a look at **ContentView.swift**. You'll see something surprising.

It's just SwiftUI code! If you've written apps for watchOS in the past, you're probably incredibly excited right now. You no longer have to use the watchOS specific classes, such as `WKInterfaceController` and `WKInterfaceLabel`, or any other UI-type class. Now, you simply write SwiftUI code, just like you do for iOS. :]

The **WatchKit** specific classes are still available and supported, but there's no reason to use them for new apps unless you need to target devices that aren't running watchOS 6.0 or newer.

Sprucing Things Up

You won't win any awards if you deploy the app as it looks now. The materials for this project include a fortune cookie image. Import that into your **HelloAppleWatch** Watch App group's assets.

Adding an Image

1. Click **Assets**.
2. Near the bottom of Xcode, click the + button to bring up a context menu.
3. Select **Import...**.
4. Navigate to this chapter's materials and select **Cookie.imageset**.

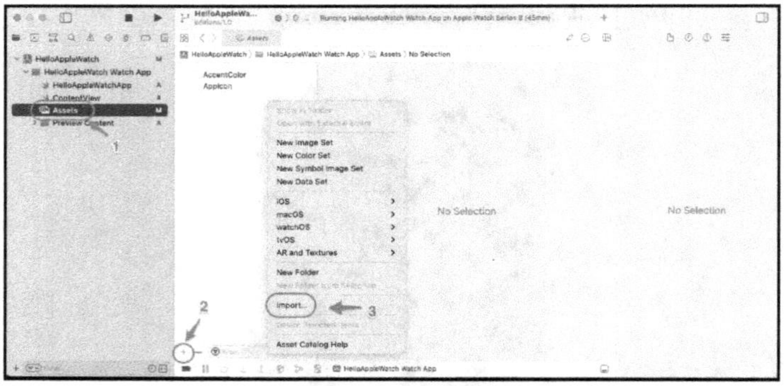

Now you have the fortune cookie image available for your app:

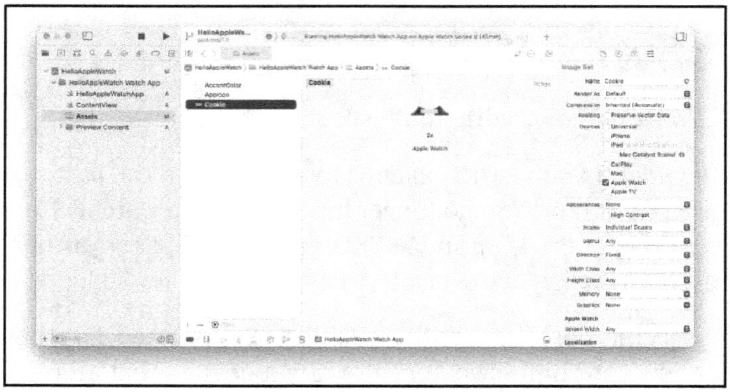

Open **ContentView** and replace the contents of `body` with:

```
VStack {
   Image("Cookie")
      .resizable()
      .scaledToFit()
}
```

Xcode's preview now shows two pieces of a fortune cookie with a blank sheet of paper between them:

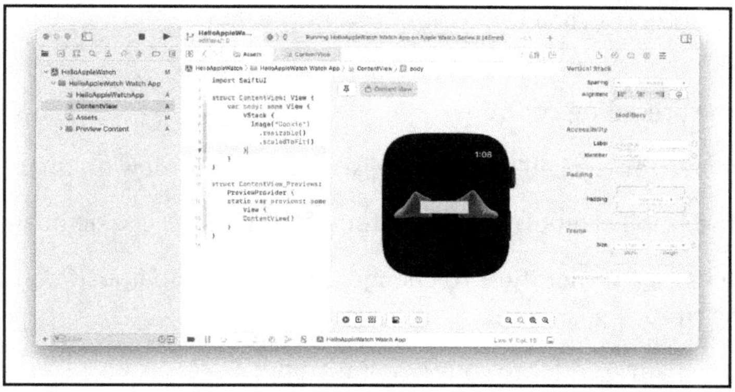

Now you need some fortunes!

Adding Fortunes

The materials for this chapter also include a file named **EmojiSentence.swift**. Add that to your project by dragging and dropping it into **HelloAppleWatch** Watch App.

Feel free to look at the code. It provides some example sentences in both English and Emoji, such as:

```
(text: "Not my cup of tea", emoji: "🙅 ☕")
```

Back in **ContentView**, add a new property to the `View`:

```
@StateObject private var sentence = EmojiSentence()
```

The `@StateObject` property wrapper ensures `sentence` is only created a single time, not each time the view's body recalculates. Add the following code just after the `.scaledToFit()` lines:

```
// 1
.overlay(
  // 2
  Text(sentence.emoji)
    // 3
    .font(.title3)
    .padding(.top, 10)
    .buttonStyle(.plain)
)
```

Here's what the preceding code does:

1. You use the `.overlay` call when you wish to layer one view on top of another.
2. You add the emoji symbols as text on top of the fortune cookie image.
3. Then, you use a few modifiers to change the font size and position to make everything fit nicely.

Build and run again. You'll see your emoji fortune:

Unfortunately, not everyone is fluent in Emoji. After the full `Image` definition, just before closing the `VStack`, add:

```
Text(sentence.text)
  .font(.caption)
  .padding(.top, 20)
```

Build and run again — or look in the Xcode preview — and you'll see the English version of the emoji text:

Getting New Fortunes

There's one last improvement to add to your app. Just after closing the `VStack`, before the end of `body`, add a tap gesture recognizer:

```
.onTapGesture { sentence.next() }
```

Build and run one final time. Tap the screen, and the fortune changes. Each time you tap, you'll receive the next fortune in the list.

But... watchOS Code?

At this point, you may be thinking that there's nothing watchOS specific here, other than the different folder structure and using the watch simulator instead of the phone simulator.

That's the whole point of this chapter! By finally supporting SwiftUI on the Apple Watch, Apple has made it much easier for you to delve into supporting watchOS. You no longer need a very specific skill set to create an Apple Watch app.

The rest of the chapters in this book will delve into development specific to the Apple Watch.

Key Points

- SwiftUI removes the need for custom frameworks to develop watchOS apps.
- Storyboards are no longer required.
- SwiftUI has been supported since watchOS 6.0.

Chapter 2: Project Structure

By Scott Grosch

You'll use Xcode when creating an app to run on the **Apple Watch**, just like when you develop for iOS. The structure is a little different, though. In iOS, you usually have a single target for the app, but you'll always have **two** when creating a watchOS app.

Start Xcode and create a new project. You'll notice some tabs at the top of the template chooser dialog. The **Multiplatform** tab is the default selection.

While you *could* start from the **App** template, you shouldn't. Instead, select the **watchOS** tab:

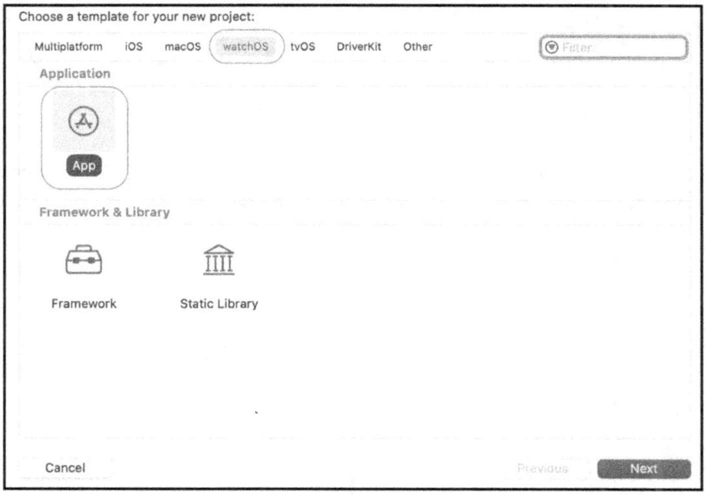

If you're reading this book, you probably need a watch app. However, what type of app are you going to create?

1. Does the watch app stand alone, with no corresponding iOS app?
2. Does the watch app require a companion iOS app to function properly?
3. Does the watch app function on its own, but there's also an iOS app?

Standalone App

Most of this book's chapters pretend that you've chosen the first option. The watch app will be fully functional and won't need a companion iOS app. As the Apple Watch is the focus of this book, I don't want to confuse the examples with a ton of code for an iOS app that doesn't add value. One of the later chapters will provide instructions for tying your Watch App to an iOS app if required.

Select the **App** template, pick a name for your project, and leave the default selection of **Watch-only App**. I chose **Standalone** for the name of the project.

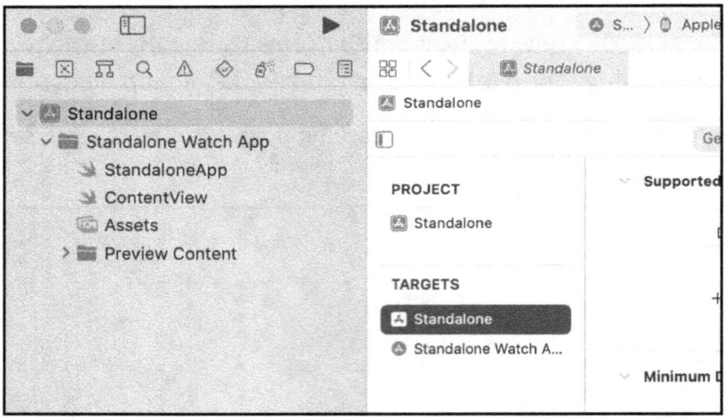

Take a look at the targets, and you'll see the template created two for you:

1. **Standalone** is the general target for your project. It acts as a wrapper for your project so that you can submit it to the App Store.
2. **Standalone Watch App** is the target for building the watchOS app. An app bundle contains your watchOS app's code and assets.

You'll seldom interact with the first target. When you think of an Apple Watch *app* you're talking about the *extension*.

Including an iOS App

If you're going to have both an iOS and a watchOS app, select the **Watch App with New Companion iOS App** option when creating a new project. You can choose any name you like — I chose **Example** — and leave the defaults for everything else. Click **Next** and choose a location. You'll get Xcode's main window.

You'll notice Xcode still provides the same two targets as before. However, this time there are directories for both the iOS app and the watchOS app. Open the scheme editor and you will see that there are two separate schemes defined. One for building and running the iOS app, and one for building and running the watchOS app.

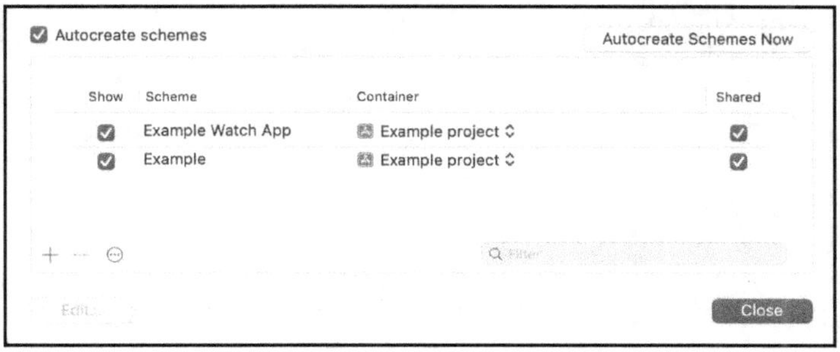

Not Requiring a Companion App

While many watchOS apps require a companion iOS project, it's also possible for a watch app to fully function without a companion iOS app. By default, Xcode assumes your watchOS app is unable to run without an installed companion iOS app.

> **Note**: Previous versions defaulted to running without requiring a companion app.

If your watch app *can* run without a corresponding iOS app, then you'll need to make a small configuration change:

1. Open the **Project Navigator** by pressing **Command-1**, and click on the project.
2. Select the watch app target.
3. Select the **General** tab.
4. In the **Deployment Info** section, check the **Supports Running Without iOS App Installation** checkbox.

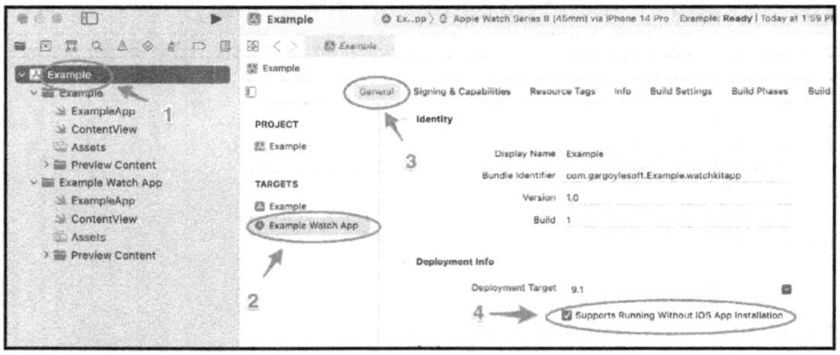

Adding Apple Watch Support Later

It's OK if you forget to include support for a watch app. Maybe you weren't ready to work on the watch app yet, or perhaps you're adding watch support to a legacy app. Maybe you just plain forgot.

With your existing iOS project open, simply add a new target via **File ▸ New ▸ Target...**, select the **watchOS** folder and then choose the **App** template. Make sure you select the radio button for **Watch App for Existing iOS App** or you may end up with a second iOS app in your project.

> **Note**: You won't be able to use the same product name for the watchOS target as the iOS target because Xcode would try to create conflicting names.

Having to pick a different name might be a hard stop for your team. If that's the case, be sure to start with the watch template instead of the iOS template.

Key Points

- Watch apps can either stand alone without an accompanying iOS app, work independently of an iOS app, or even require an iOS app.
- You can add watch support to an iOS app at a later date.

Chapter 3: Digital Crown

By Scott Grosch

In the starter materials for this chapter, please open the **NumberScroller** project. Build and run the project. You'll see a lonely number:

Scrolling the **Digital Crown** makes it easy for your users to edit a number's value, such as the one shown.

If you're debugging with a physical device, rotate the crown. If you're debugging on the simulator, scrolling your mouse simulates turning the digital crown. Give it a spin, and watch the number change.

Binding a Value

Did nothing happen? That shouldn't come as much of a surprise since you didn't tell watchOS what to do when you rotated the crown.

To let the Digital Crown interact with a SwiftUI control, you use `digitalCrownRotation`. It takes a ridiculous number of parameters in its full form, but you'll start with just one.

Open **ContentView**. Modify the `Text` field as follows:

```
Text("\(number, specifier: "%.1f")")
  .focusable()
  .digitalCrownRotation($number)
```

By default, a `Text` field won't accept focus as it's not an interactive element. When using the `digitalCrownRotation` modifier, typically you'll also immediately precede the call with `.focusable()`, so watchOS lets you interact with the view you're modifying.

`digitalCrownRotation` always takes a binding as the first parameter to anything which implements the `BinaryFloatingPoint` protocol, such as a `Double`. Build and run again. This time, when you scroll the Digital Crown, you'll see the number change.

Limiting the Scroll Range

Generally, having the number scroll infinitely in either direction isn't what you'll want to accomplish. You can limit the range of values by adding two more parameters.

Update your method call like so:

```
.digitalCrownRotation($number, from: 0.0, through: 12.0)
```

You specified a lower limit of `0.0` and an upper limit of `12.0`. Build and run the project. You'll see some surprising results.

Scrolling all the way in either direction displays a lower value of `-0.1` and an upper value of `12.1`. When using ranges, you must add one more parameter to tell the Digital Crown how much to change the value.

Now, update the method call again:

```
.digitalCrownRotation($number, from: 0.0, through: 12.0, by:
0.1)
```

Build and run again. This time, you'll get the results you were expecting.

> **Note**: Always include the `by:` parameter when specifying `from:` and `through:`. That way there is no doubt of what the expected behavior is.

The Joys of Floating-Point

Remember that a floating-point value is seldom *exactly* what you expect it to be. The OS tracks floating-point to many more decimal places than a human does. To see what the Digital Crown is doing, add this right before `.focusable()`:

```
.onChange(of: number) { print($0) }
```

`onChange(of:perform:)` lets you display a property's new value any time it changes. Activate Xcode's console by pressing **Shift-Command-C**. Then build and run yet again.

As you scroll the Digital Crown, you'll see output like this in the console:

```
9.741019864982159.7356469082736249.7309777243314469.726920129971415
9.700000000000001
```

There are two main takeaways from that output:

1. The bound property updates with many more values than you'd assume.
2. The bound property is usually, but not *always*, limited by the `by:` parameter when rotation stops.

The first point doesn't matter in an app like the one you're currently working on since the display formats the value as you'd expect. The user will never see those intermediate values.

What *is* important to keep in mind is the second point. When the Digital Crown stops moving, you might have a value of `9.700000000000001` instead of the expected `9.7`. Depending on what you've bound the Digital Crown's value to, that may or may not make a difference.

If you need to perform an equality check against a floating point number, use the `rounded` method, like this:

```
if (value * 10).rounded(.towardZero) / 10 == 9.7 {
  ...
}
```

`rounded(.towardZero)` rounds the value provided to an integral value by always rounding toward zero. You multiply and divide by ten to the power of **X**, where **X** is the number of decimal places you're comparing against.

In the example, `9.7` has a single decimal place, so you compare against 10. If you were comparing against `9.78`, then it's two decimal places, thus `10 ^ 2`, or 100.

Sensitivity

When scrolling the Digital Crown, you can specify how sensitive the update should be. Think of the sensitivity as how much you need to scroll the crown for a change to take effect. Add another parameter:

```
.digitalCrownRotation(
  $number,
  from: 0.0,
  through: 12.0,
  by: 0.1,
  sensitivity: .high
)
```

Build and run, paying attention to how much you have to turn the Digital Crown to scroll through the full range. Next, change the value from `.high` to `.medium` and try again. Finally, change `.medium` to `.low` and try a final time.

When the value is `.low`, you'll notice you have to turn the Digital Crown quite a bit more than when you set the value to `.high`. The default value is `.high`.

Wrapping Around

Until now, when you reached the `from` or `through` values, the number stopped changing. You could continue turning the Digital Crown, but it wouldn't make any updates.

For a number range, stopping makes sense. In other scenarios, where the actual value isn't visible to the end-user, wrapping the value around to the starting value might make sense.

In other words, you can scroll up to 12, as normal, but if you keep scrolling the value goes to 0 and starts climbing again. Apple calls this **continuous scrolling**. The default is `false`, but you can enable it by adding another parameter:

```
.digitalCrownRotation(
  $number,
  from: 0.0,
  through: 12.0,
  by: 0.1,
  sensitivity: .high,
  isContinuous: true
)
```

Build and run again. Continuously scroll the Digital Crown, and you'll see the numbers wrap around repeatedly.

Haptic Feedback

By default, scrolling the Digital Crown provides a small amount of haptic feedback to the user. If that doesn't make sense for your app, you can turn it off by using the final parameter to the `digitalCrownRotation` call:

```
.digitalCrownRotation(
  $number,
  from: 0.0,
  through: 12.0,
  by: 0.1,
  sensitivity: .high,
  isContinuous: true,
  isHapticFeedbackEnabled: false
)
```

> **Note**: The simulator never provides haptic feedback. :]

Pong

While scrolling numbers is super fun, you won't always show the actual numeric value to your app's user.

In 1972, Atari released **Pong**, the first commercially successful video game. At the time, it was groundbreaking. Show it to your kids today... I dare you. :]

Each player controlled a paddle that only moved up and down to block an incoming ball. Seems like a perfect use case for the Digital Crown to me!

Open **Pong.xcodeproj** from this project's starter materials. Then build and run, preparing yourself for a visual feast:

While clearly a gorgeous app, you currently have no way to move the paddle, so the player on the left scores continuously. Time to fix that.

Hooking Up the Digital Crown

Open **ContentView**. You'll see that Pong is implemented as a **SpriteKit** game. The `SpriteView(scene:)` initializer makes adding a SpriteKit scene to your SwiftUI app easy. To provide the scene's size to SpriteKit, the `SpriteView` is wrapped in a `GeometryReader`.

You need to link the `crownPosition` to the value of the Digital Crown. Add these two modifiers right after the `SpriteView` line:

```
.focusable()
.digitalCrownRotation($crownPosition)
```

In this case, you don't need any of the numerous options available on the `.digitalCrownRotation` call. All that matters is you constantly update the value of `crownPosition`. The SpriteKit scene will handle the bounds checking. Your `ContentView` shouldn't know or care about the scene's logic.

Now that you've linked the Digital Crown to the scene, it's time to move those paddles.

Paddle Movement

Open **PongScene**, which implements all of the SpriteKit scene logic. Scroll down to the overridden `update(_:)`. SpriteKit will call `update(_:)` once per frame before it simulates any actions or physics.

Your goal is to have the defender's paddle move in reaction to the user rotating the Digital Crown. Movement means an action taking place, so `update(_:)` is the proper location to respond to the Digital Crown's value changing.

First, you need to determine whether the user rotated the Digital Crown since the last frame update. At the end of the method, add:

```
let newPosition = crownPosition

// 1
defer { previousCrownPosition = newPosition }

// 2
guard newPosition != previousCrownPosition else { return }
```

Here's what the code does:

1. Regardless of why you exit the method, the code ensures the current crown position reflects as `previousCrownPosition` on the next update.
2. If there's no change, you exit the method right away to keep performance as fast as possible.

Once you know the paddle needs to move, assign a new position by adding this code to the end of the method:

```
// 1
let offset = newPosition - previousCrownPosition
let y = paddleBeingMoved.position.y + offset

// 2
guard minPaddleY ... maxPaddleY ~= y else { return }

// 3
paddleBeingMoved.position.y = y
```

In the preceding code, you:

1. Calculate the amount by which the user scrolled the Digital Crown, storing the paddle's new location.
2. Perform bounds checking on the paddle's location. The scene knows the minimum and maximum y values, so if you continue to turn the Digital Crown, the paddle doesn't leave the game zone.
3. Everything is copacetic, so you tell the paddle about its new location.

The operators used in step two may be unfamiliar to you. The `...` range operator works similarly to the more familiar `..<` operator. The difference is the former includes the final value, whereas the latter doesn't. Using a range operator with the contains operator (~=) lets you determine if a value is in the range.

Step two is a more concise syntax for this equivalent code:

```
guard y >= minPaddleY && y <= maxPaddleY else {
  return
}
```

Build and run again.You should now have a playable Pong video game in your wrist!

> **Note**: This was my first ever SpriteKit project. If you're a professional game developer, try not to cringe too much. :]

Key Points

- Remember to add the `focusable` method modifier when using the Digital Crown.
- If you need to compare two floating-point values for equality, use the `rounded(.towardZero)` method.

Chapter 4: Watch Connectivity

By Scott Grosch

The magic of the Apple Watch experience comes from seamless interactions between the watch and your iOS apps.

> **Note**: This is the first chapter that requires the app to run on **both** the Apple Watch and iPhone at the same time. While this setup is possible by starting both simulators from Xcode, the connectivity mechanisms you'll use in this chapter rarely work between them. You may need to run the example projects on real devices to see them in action. Even if you don't have the hardware, it's still a good read.

Watch Connectivity, an Apple-provided framework, lets an iOS app and its counterpart watchOS app transfer data and files back and forth. If both apps are active, communication occurs *mostly* in real time. Otherwise, communication happens in the background, so data is available as soon as the receiving app launches.

The OS takes many factors into account when determining exactly how quickly to pass data packets between devices. While the transfers frequently happen within a matter of moments, sometimes you'll see a significant lag.

Be aware, to transfer data between devices, multiple system resources, such as Bluetooth, must be on. This can result in significant energy use.

> **Note**: Bundle messages together whenever possible to limit battery consumption.

In this chapter, after learning about the different types of messaging options, you'll implement data transfers between the iPhone and Apple Watch versions of **CinemaTime**, an app for patrons of a fictional theater. It lets customers view movie showtimes and buy tickets right from their iPhones and Apple Watches.

Device-to-Device Communication

The Watch Connectivity framework provides five different methods for transferring data between devices. Four of those methods send arbitrary data, while the fifth sends files between devices. All of the methods are part of `WCSession`.

> **Note**: Although most data transfer methods accept a dictionary of type `[String: Any]`, this doesn't mean you can send just anything. The dictionary can only accept primitive types. See the Property List Programming Guide (http://apple.co/1PZEPXD), for a complete list of supported types.

Those five methods are further subdivided into two categories: interactive messaging and background transfers.

Interactive Messaging

Interactive messaging works best in situations where you need to transfer information immediately. For example, if a watchOS app needs to trigger the iOS app to check the user's current location, the interactive messaging API can transfer the request from the Apple Watch to the iPhone.

However, remember there's no guarantee that interactive messages will be delivered. They're sent as soon as possible and delivered asynchronously in **first-in, first-out**, or **FIFO**, order.

If you send an interactive message from your watchOS app, the corresponding iOS app will wake in the background and become reachable.When you send an interactive message from your iOS app, and the watch app isn't active, the watchOS app will **not** wake up.

If you have a dictionary of data, keyed by string, use `sendMessage(_:replyHandler:errorHandler:)`. If, instead, you have a `Data` object, then use `sendMessageData(_:replyHandler:errorHandler:)`.

Reply Handlers

When sending an interactive message, you probably expect a reply from the peer device. You may pass a closure of type `([String: Any]) -> Void` as the `replyHandler`, which will receive the message that the peer device sends back.

If you ask the iPhone to generate some type of data, the message will return to the `replyHandler`.

Error Handlers

When you wish to know when something goes wrong during a message transfer, you can use the `errorHandler` and pass a `(Error) -> Void`. For example, you'd call the handler if the network fails.

Background Transfers

If only one of the apps is active, it can still send data to its counterpart app using background transfer methods.

Background transfers let iOS and watchOS choose a good time to transfer data between apps, based on characteristics such as battery use and how much other data is waiting to transfer.

There are three types of background transfers:

- Guaranteed user information
- Application context
- Files

Guaranteed User Information

`transferUserInfo(_:)` makes the first type of background transfer. When calling this method, you specify the data is critical and must be delivered as soon as possible.

The device will continue to attempt to send the data until the peer device receives it. Once the data transfer beings, the operation will continue even if the app suspends.

`transferUserInfo(_:)` delivers every data packet you send in a FIFO manner.

Next, you'll take a look at a similar type of background transfer, application context.

Application Context, aka High Priority User Information

High priority messages, delivered via `updateApplicationContext(_:)`, are similar to guaranteed user information with two important differences:

1. The OS sends the data when it feels it's appropriate to send it.

2. It only sends the most recent message.

If you have data that updates frequently, and you only need the most recent data, you should use `updateApplicationContext(_:)`.

Here are a few examples of when application context makes sense:

- Sending the most recent score in a game. The paired device only needs the most up-to-date score.
- Updating the Apple Watch's dock image.
- A gas-finding app might send updates on prices. It doesn't matter what the gas *used* to cost. You only need the current price.

While guaranteed user information and high priority message work for some situations, you need a different approach with files.

Files

Sometimes you need to send actual files between devices, as opposed to just data. For example, the iPhone might download an image from the network and then send that image to the Apple Watch.

You send a file via `transferFile(_:metadata:)`. You can send any type of dictionary data, keyed by `String`, via the **metadata** parameter. Use metadata to provide information like the file's name, size and when it was created.

Now you're ready to get started.

Getting Started

Open the **CinemaTime** starter project in Xcode. Then build and run the **CinemaTime** scheme. The simulator for the iPhone will appear.

Now build and run the **CinemaTime Watch App** scheme to start the Apple Watch simulator.

Take a moment to compare the two apps.

Compare and Contrast

In the Apple Watch simulator, tap **Purchase Tickets.** Explore the app to see what you have to work with:

Now switch to the iPhone simulator and do the same thing:

While the initial screen looks pretty similar, there are a few noticeable differences on the second screen:

- The iPhone version's grouped list items are collapsible, whereas the watchOS version is not.
- The iPhone includes the movie's poster. There's no room on the Apple Watch to display a poster.
- The Apple Watch version doesn't include details about the movie.

While you *could* include a poster on the Apple Watch version, the image would be so small your customers wouldn't gain any benefit from having it. More importantly, including an image would mean the movie title would have to be even smaller to still fit in a decent amount of space.

The phone has plenty of space to include a short synopsis of the movie, but the Apple Watch doesn't. If you were to include the synopsis, then the person running your app would have to scroll quite a bit more than they likely want to.

Explore the app further by placing an order.

Place Your Order

Buy a movie ticket in either app. Then view the list of purchased movie tickets in the other app. Do you see the issue?

Movie tickets purchased on one device don't show as purchased on the other device! The apps aren't transferring ticket purchase data between them. Imagine if a customer bought a movie ticket in the iPhone app, then tried to use the Apple Watch app to get into the theater. They'd be turned away, as the Apple Watch wouldn't have a ticket!

Customers have a reasonable expectation that data should be accessible from both versions of an app regardless of which app created the data.

In the rest of this chapter, you'll use the **Watch Connectivity** framework to sync the customer's purchased movie tickets between the iOS and watchOS versions of the app.

First, you'll set up watch connectivity.

Setting Up Watch Connectivity

You should handle all connectivity between your devices from a single location in your code. Hopefully, the term **singleton** comes to mind!

The code you write will be nearly the same for both iOS and watchOS. So, under the **Shared** folder, create a new file called **Connectivity** with the following contents:

```
import Foundation
// 1
import WatchConnectivity

final class Connectivity {
  // 2
  static let shared = Connectivity()

  // 3
  private init() {
    // 4
    #if !os(watchOS)
    guard WCSession.isSupported() else {
      return
    }
    #endif

    // 5
    WCSession.default.activate()
  }
}
```

Here's a code breakdown:

1. You must include the `WatchConnectivity` framework.
2. Use `static` to access singletons.
3. Ensure the initializer is `private` so the class is only accessible via `shared`.
4. You should only start a session if it's supported. An Apple Watch will always support a session. An iOS device will only support a session if there's a paired Apple Watch.
5. When you initialize `Connectivity`, you tell the device to activate the session, which lets you talk to a paired device.

> **Note**: You don't have to wrap the `isSupported` call in an OS check, but I like to make it clear when something is only necessary on a certain type of device.

Be sure to add the file to the target membership of both the iOS app and the extension in the file inspector. Press **Option-Command-1** to bring up the **File Inspector**.

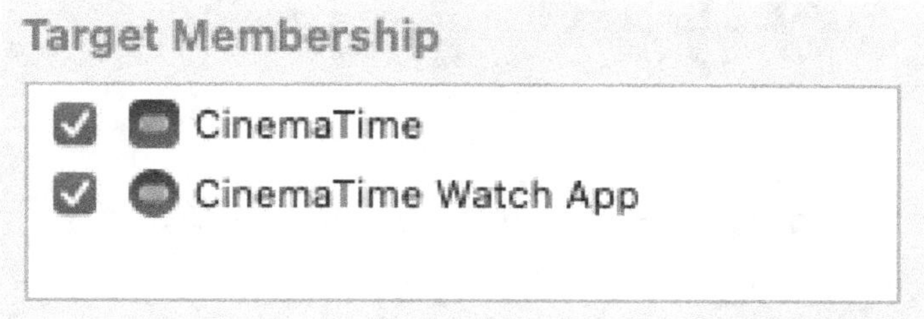

If you were to run the above code right now, you'd receive an error log message. The documentation explicitly says that activating a session without a delegate is a no-no. So, you'll fix that now!

Preparing for WCSessionDelegate

The `WCSessionDelegate` protocol extends `NSObjectProtocol`. That means for `Connectivity` to be the delegate, it must inherit from `NSObject`.

Change the class declaration to this:

```
final class Connectivity: NSObject {
```

As soon as you subclass from `NSObject`, you'll receive a compiler error on the initializer. Since you've subclassed, you have to override the initializer and call the parent's initializer. Change the init you already have to start like this:

```
override private init() {
  super.init()
```

Next, you'll implement the delegate.

Implementing WCSessionDelegate

You need to make `Connectivity` conform to `WCSessionDelegate`. At the bottom of the file, add:

```
// MARK: - WCSessionDelegate
extension Connectivity: WCSessionDelegate {
  func session(
      _ session: WCSession,
      activationDidCompleteWith activationState:
WCSessionActivationState,
      error: Error?
  ) {
  }

  func sessionDidBecomeInactive(_ session: WCSession) {
  }

  func sessionDidDeactivate(_ session: WCSession) {
  }
}
```

Almost immediately, you'll receive compiler errors on the last two methods. Those methods are part of the delegate on iOS, but they're *not* present in watchOS.

Since the methods are only valid for iOS, wrap them in a compiler check:

```
#if os(iOS)
func sessionDidBecomeInactive(_ session: WCSession) {
}

func sessionDidDeactivate(_ session: WCSession) {
}
#endif
```

While it may boggle the mind, some people have more than one Apple Watch! If the user swaps watches, the session will deactivate. Apple suggests when the session deactivates, simply restart it. That covers the case of swapping watches.

Add these lines to `sessionDidDeactivate(_:)`:

```
// If the person has more than one watch, and they switch,
// reactivate their session on the new device.
WCSession.default.activate()
```

Now jump back up to `init` and mark the class as the delegate on the line right before calling `WCSession.default.activate()`:

```
WCSession.default.delegate = self
```

Now that you've established a connection, you need some way to send a message to the paired device.

Sending Messages

In the class, add:

```
public func send(movieIds: [Int]) {
  guard WCSession.default.activationState == .activated else {
    return
  }
}
```

Whenever you purchase a ticket to a new movie or delete a ticket, you'll want to tell the companion app which movies are now valid. Whenever sending a message, the first thing you must do is ensure the session is active.

Remember, the session state could change for any number of reasons. For example, one device's battery might die, or the user might be in the middle of swapping watches.

Notice how there are no errors when the session isn't active. There's nothing to do, and you don't want to display a confusing message to your end-user.

In Chapter 2, "Project Structure", you learned that a watchOS app doesn't always need a companion iOS app, and vice versa. That means, before sending any message, you need to verify the peer device is there.

Add the following code to your `send(movieIds:)`:

```
// 1
#if os(watchOS)
// 2
guard WCSession.default.isCompanionAppInstalled else {
  return
}
#else
// 3
guard WCSession.default.isWatchAppInstalled else {
  return
}
#endif
```

There are three key points to note in the above code:

1. You use a compiler check to ensure you call the proper method.
2. The Apple Watch checks if the app is on the phone. If it's not, there's nothing else to do.
3. The iOS device checks if the app is on the Apple Watch. If it's not, there's nothing else to do.

Unfortunately, due to legacy watchOS code, the two operating systems have separately named methods.

Now that you've found an active session with your app installed on both devices, it's time to send the data. Add these lines to the end of the method you're working on:

```
// 1
let userInfo: [String: [Int]] = [
  ConnectivityUserInfoKey.purchased.rawValue: movieIds
]

// 2
WCSession.default.transferUserInfo(userInfo)
```

Here's a code breakdown:

1. When sending data to a paired device, you must use a dictionary keyed by a string. The sample project includes an `enum` to specify which keys are valid for transfers, so you don't hardcode strings.
2. Once the data is ready, you can transfer it to the paired device.

Refer back to the start of this chapter, and you'll likely conclude that `transferUserInfo(_:)` is the wrong method to use. You're correct!

Before the end of the chapter, you'll use each type of connectivity and build out a mostly generic connectivity class you can use as a base in all your projects.

Receiving Messages

After transferring the user information, you need some way to receive it on the other device. You'll receive the data in the `WCSessionDelegate` of `session(_:didReceiveUserInfo:)`. Using the Combine framework is a great way to let your app know about the updates.

Modify your class to implement `ObservableObject`, and then add a publisher:

```
final class Connectivity: NSObject, ObservableObject {
  @Published var purchasedIds: [Int] = []
```

> **Note**: You can learn more about `@Published` in our RW book: *Combine: Asynchronous Programming with Swift (*https://bit.ly/3y8Ot5o).

Using `@Published`, you enable other parts of your program to observe changes to `purchasedIds`.

Add the following method to the delegate extension:

```
// 1
func session(
  _ session: WCSession,
  didReceiveUserInfo userInfo: [String: Any] = [:]
) {
  // 2
  let key = ConnectivityUserInfoKey.purchased.rawValue
  guard let ids = userInfo[key] as? [Int] else {
    return
  }

  // 3
  self.purchasedIds = ids
}
```

Here's a code breakdown:

1. When transferring data via `transferUserInfo(_:)`, you receive it via the aptly named `session(_:didReceiveUserInfo:)`.
2. Check to see if the provided user information contains a list of purchased movie keys. If not, quietly do nothing.
3. Assigning to `purchasedIds` automatically notifies all observers about the change.

Build your project to ensure you aren't missing anything at this point. You won't get any errors or warnings, but you can't run yet as there's still nothing visible to see. Almost there!

The Ticket Office

When you purchase or delete a ticket, you need to let companion devices know. **Shared/TicketOffice** handles purchasing and deleting tickets, so it seems like a good place to handle connectivity! Open that file.

Look through it. You'll see both `purchase(_:)` and `delete(at:)`. These methods need to send a message to the companion app.

Since you would never consider duplicating code, add a private method to the bottom of the file:

```
private func updateCompanion() {
  // 1
  let ids = purchased.map { $0.id }

  // 2
  Connectivity.shared.send(movieIds: ids)
}
```

In the preceding code:

1. There's no need to transfer entire Movie objects between devices. Instead, you grab the ID of each ticket you've purchased.
2. Using your newly created Connectivity, you send the data to the other device.

Add a call to updateCompanion() as the last step in both delete(at:) and purchase(_:).

You're now sending and receiving ticket purchase updates. However, if you build and run the app at this point, the tickets still won't update. Why not?

Look at **PurchasedTicketsListView** in either the iOS or watchOS target. You'll see the list of tickets comes from the purchased property of TicketOffice. Update the TicketOffice initializer to include the following code at the end of the method:

```
// 1
Connectivity.shared.$purchasedIds
  // 2
  .dropFirst()
  // 3
  .map { ids in movies.filter { ids.contains($0.id) }}
  // 4
  .receive(on: DispatchQueue.main)
  // 5
  .assign(to: \.purchased, on: self)
  //6
  .store(in: &cancellable)
```

That's quite the chain of calls! If you're not familiar with the Combine framework, that probably looks pretty scary. Here's a line-by-line breakdown:

1. By prefacing the property with `$`, you tell Swift to look at the publishing item rather than just the value.
2. You declared `purchasedIds` with an initial value of `[]`, meaning an empty array. By dropping the first item, you essentially skip the empty assignment.
3. Next, you retrieve `Movie` objects identified by the IDs sent to the device. Performing the inner filter ensures an ID sent for a movie that doesn't exist doesn't throw an error.
4. Because you'll use the list of purchased movies to update the user interface, you switch over to the main thread. Always make UI updates on the main thread!
5. Now that you've created a list of `Movie` objects, assign that to `purchased`.
6. Finally, include the standard boilerplate for Combine, which stores the chain in `Set<AnyCancellable>`.

It's the moment of truth! Build and run the updated app on both devices. Then purchase a ticket on the phone.

After a few moments, the Apple Watch will update.

> **Note**: Remember, updates can take some time. While writing this book, I saw the iPhone update the Apple Watch almost immediately, whereas the watch sometimes updated the phone three minutes or so later.

Application Context

While functional, using `transferUserInfo(:_)` isn't the best choice for **CinemaTime**. If you purchase a movie ticket on one device, you don't need to see it immediately on the other device. Unless you're standing right outside the theater, it's OK if the transfer happens later. Even if you *are* outside the theater, you'd still use the device you purchased the ticket on.

In this case, the best choice is to use `updateApplicationContext(_:)`. You need the message to arrive, so none of the `sendMessage` variants would make sense.

Add a new file named **Shared/Delivery** with the following contents:

```
enum Delivery {
  /// Deliver immediately. No retries on failure.
  case failable

  /// Deliver as soon as possible. Automatically retries on
failure.
  /// All instances of the data will be transferred
sequentially.
  case guaranteed

  /// High priority data like app settings. Only the most recent
value is
  /// used. Any transfers of this type not yet delivered will be
replaced
  /// with the new one.
  case highPriority
}
```

> **Note**: Remember to update the target membership to include both the iOS app **and** the watchOS extension.

You'll use that `enum` to specify the type of delivery the caller wants to use. I chose the labels I did because they make more sense to me. `guaranteed` and `highPriority` make sense to me when I glance at code later, instead of trying to remember whether it was a user information transfer or an updated application context guaranteed to arrive quickly.

Now jump back to **Shared/Connectivity**. Add a couple of extra parameters to the send method:

```
public func send(
  movieIds: [Int],
  delivery: Delivery,
  errorHandler: ((Error) -> Void)? = nil
) {
```

Now you can specify both the type of delivery you'd like to use as well as an optional error handler.

Then, at the bottom of that method, replace the call to `transferUserInfo(_:)` with:

```
switch delivery {
case .failable:
  break

case .guaranteed:
  WCSession.default.transferUserInfo(userInfo)

case .highPriority:
  do {
    try WCSession.default.updateApplicationContext(userInfo)
  } catch {
    errorHandler?(error)
  }
}
```

You'll handle the `.failable` case in a moment. In the case of a high-priority delivery, there's a new wrinkle to handle.

Updating the application context might throw an exception, which is why the send method now accepts an optional error handler.

> **Note**: Remember, you call the session delegate methods on a background thread, so be kind to your consumers and dispatch back to the main queue for them.

In the delegate, you need to receive the application context like you received user information. Since the code is going to be the same, do a quick bit of refactoring.

Extract the contents of `session(_:didReceiveUserInfo:)` into a private method:

```
private func update(from dictionary: [String: Any]) {
  let key = ConnectivityUserInfoKey.purchased.rawValue
  guard let ids = dictionary[key] as? [Int] else {
    return
  }

  self.purchasedIds = ids
}
```

Then call it from the delegate method:

```
func session(
  _ session: WCSession,
  didReceiveUserInfo userInfo: [String: Any] = [:]
) {
  update(from: userInfo)
}
```

Also call it from a new delegate method for receiving the application context:

```
func session(
  _ session: WCSession,
  didReceiveApplicationContext applicationContext: [String: Any]
) {
  update(from: applicationContext)
}
```

Switch back to **Shared/TicketOffice** and replace the connectivity call in `updateCompanion()` with:

```
Connectivity.shared.send(movieIds: ids, delivery: .highPriority,
errorHandler: {
  print($0.localizedDescription)
})
```

Now, when a user purchases a ticket, you'll use the application context transference method instead. A production app would, however, likely want to do something better than just printing to the console in case of an error.

Optional Messages

Remember, interactive messages might fail to send. While that makes them inappropriate for the CinemaTime app, you'll make the appropriate updates to `Connectivity` to support them so you can reuse the code later.

It's a bit trickier to deal with interactive messages. They take an optional reply handler and an optional error handler. If you can't send the message or ask for a reply and can't receive it, the error handler is called.

The most common reason for an error is when the paired device isn't reachable, but other errors are possible.

> **Note**: Remember, if you're not expecting a reply from the peer device, you *must* pass `nil` as the reply handler when calling `sendMessage(_:replyHandler:errorHandler:)`. If you pass a closure to the parameter, you tell the OS you expect a reply, and it should generate an error if one isn't received.

Also, don't directly pass `replyHandler` and `errorHandler` from your custom send method, as the handlers would then run on a background thread, not the main thread.

How do you handle both situations? With the addition of a small helper function to **Shared/Connectivity**. It's quite clean.

Add this to the end of the `Connectivity` class:

```
// 1
typealias OptionalHandler<T> = ((T) -> Void)?

// 2
private func optionalMainQueueDispatch<T>(handler:
OptionalHandler<T>) -> OptionalHandler<T> {
  // 3
  guard let handler = handler else {
    return nil
  }

  // 4
  return { item in
    // 5
    Task { @MainActor in
      handler(item)
    }
  }
}
```

There are a ton of powerful features here in a few lines of code. Here's a breakdown:

1. While not strictly necessary, using `typealias` makes the rest of the code easier to read. You create an alias for an optional method that takes a single generic parameter `T` and has no return value.
2. You declare a method of that same `T` type and take an optional handler. Remember that `OptionalHandler<T>` is already optional, so you don't add `?` to the end of the type.
3. If no handler was provided, then return `nil`.
4. The return type is an `OptionalHandler<T>`, meaning you need to return a closure to represent the call. The closure will take a single item of type `T`, as expected by the definition of the type.
5. You dispatch the provided handler to the main thread using the delivered data.

It's quite a bit to wrap your head around if you've never returned a closure from another method. So, don't be afraid to work through the code a few times to be sure you understand it.

Non-Binary Data

Optional messages might or might not expect a reply from the peer device. So, add a new `replyHandler` to your send method in **Shared/Connectivity** so it looks like this:

```
public func send(
  movieIds: [Int],
  delivery: Delivery,
  replyHandler: (([String: Any]) -> Void)? = nil,
  errorHandler: ((Error) -> Void)? = nil
) {
```

Now it's time to enjoy the fruits of your labor. Replace the `break` statement in the `.failable` case with the following:

```
WCSession.default.sendMessage(
  userInfo,
  replyHandler: optionalMainQueueDispatch(handler:
replyHandler),
  errorHandler: optionalMainQueueDispatch(handler: errorHandler)
)
```

By implementing `optionalMainQueueDispatch(_:)`, you keep a clean `case` that handles all the complexities of passing a handler vs. `nil`. You also ensure that both handlers, if provided, are called on the main thread.

Technically, you'd be OK always providing an error handler. But why make the OS perform the extra work of configuring and dispatching an error if you're going to ignore it anyway?

To handle receiving messages, add two separate delegate methods:

```
// This method is called when a message is sent with failable
priority
// *and* a reply was requested.
func session(
  _ session: WCSession,
  didReceiveMessage message: [String: Any],
  replyHandler: @escaping ([String: Any]) -> Void
) {
  update(from: message)

  let key = ConnectivityUserInfoKey.verified.rawValue
  replyHandler([key: true])
}

// This method is called when a message is sent with failable
priority
// and a reply was *not* requested.
func session(
  _ session: WCSession,
  didReceiveMessage message: [String: Any]
) {
  update(from: message)
}
```

It's unfortunate, but Apple implemented two completely separate delegate methods instead of having one with an optional reply handler. In both instances, you'll call `update(from:)`, just like in the other delegate methods you've added so far.

The only difference is that in the delegate method which expects to send a reply back to the other device, you have to invoke the provided handler. The data you send back is arbitrary. For this example, you send back a `true` response.

Binary Data

Optional messages can also transfer binary data. It's unclear why only optional messages provide a binary option.

You'll need a separate sending method in `Connectivity` to handle the `Data` type. As you coded it, you'd quickly see that both methods need all the same `guard` clauses. So, refactor them into a method of their own:

```
private func canSendToPeer() -> Bool {
  guard WCSession.default.activationState == .activated else {
    return false
  }

  #if os(watchOS)
  guard WCSession.default.isCompanionAppInstalled else {
    return false
  }
  #else
  guard WCSession.default.isWatchAppInstalled else {
    return false
  }
  #endif

  return true
}
```

Those are the same checks you performed previously. Now, you move them to a method that returns `true` when you can send.

Remove those guard clauses from `send(movieIds:delivery:replyHandler:errorHandler:)` and replace them with a call to the new method:

```
guard canSendToPeer() else { return }
```

Now you can implement the method to handle binary data:

```
public func send(
  data: Data,
  replyHandler: ((Data) -> Void)? = nil,
  errorHandler: ((Error) -> Void)? = nil
) {
  guard canSendToPeer() else { return }

  WCSession.default.sendMessageData(
    data,
    replyHandler: optionalMainQueueDispatch(handler:
replyHandler),
    errorHandler: optionalMainQueueDispatch(handler:
errorHandler)
  )
}
```

Receiving binary data, of course, results in two more delegate methods:

```
func session(
  _ session: WCSession,
  didReceiveMessageData messageData: Data
) {
}

func session(
  _ session: WCSession,
  didReceiveMessageData messageData: Data,
  replyHandler: @escaping (Data) -> Void
) {
}
```

I haven't provided a sample implementation as that would be specific to the type of binary data your app is transferring.

Transferring Files

If you run the app on your iOS device and purchase a ticket, you'll notice that the movie details include a QR code. Ostensibly, that QR code is what the theater would scan to grant entry. Purchasing a ticket on the Apple Watch, however, does not display a QR code.

You'll see a file called **CinemaTime/QRCode** that generates the QR code using the **CoreImage** library. Unfortunately, CoreImage does not exist in watchOS.

An image like this is an excellent example wherein you might opt to use file transfers. When you purchase a ticket on the Apple Watch, the iOS device gets a message with the new movie list. Wouldn't that be a great time to ask the iOS device to generate a QR code and send it back?

> **Note**: When debugging file transfer issues, consider using the `.failable` delivery type, so the transfer is attempted immediately.

QR Codes

Move **CinemaTime/QRCode** into **Shared**. Then add the watch app to the target membership. To fix the error that immediately appears, wrap both the import of CoreImage and `generate(movie:size:)` in a compiler check:

```
import SwiftUI
#if canImport(CoreImage)
import CoreImage.CIFilterBuiltins
#endif

enum QRCode {
  #if canImport(CoreImage)
  static func generate(movie: Movie, size: CGSize) -> UIImage? {
    // Code removed for brevity. [...]
  }
  #endif
}
```

When the Apple Watch displays the details of a purchased ticket, it needs to know where to look for the QR code's image. Add a helper method to the `enum` but *outside* the `canImport` check:

```
#if os(watchOS)
static func url(for movieId: Int) -> URL {
  let documents = FileManager.default.urls(
    for: .documentDirectory,
    in: .userDomainMask
  )[0]

  return documents.appendingPathComponent("\(movieId).png")
}
#endif
```

iOS doesn't need to look at a file URL, but watchOS does. The preceding code gets the path to the app's documents directory and then appends the movie's ID to the path.

> **Note**: If you don't name the file with a `.png` suffix, then the OS will refuse to turn that file into an image.

Open **Shared/Connectivity** and edit `send(movieIds:delivery:replyHandler:errorHandler:)` to add `wantedQrCodes`:

```
public func send(
  movieIds: [Int],
  delivery: Delivery,
  wantedQrCodes: [Int]? = nil,
  replyHandler: (([String: Any]) -> Void)? = nil,
  errorHandler: ((Error) -> Void)? = nil
) {
```

Then, change `userInfo` from a `let` to a `var` and assign the wanted QR codes:

```
var userInfo: [String: [Int]] = [
  ConnectivityUserInfoKey.purchased.rawValue: movieIds
]

if let wantedQrCodes {
  let key = ConnectivityUserInfoKey.qrCodes.rawValue
  userInfo[key] = wantedQrCodes
}
```

That provides a way for the Apple Watch to request a QR code for a list of movies from the iOS device. Why a list instead of just one ID? The previous request to deliver an image might have failed for any number of possible reasons.

Now you can implement the method that will run on the iOS device to generate and send the QR code images. Add this code to the end of `Connectivity`:

```
#if os(iOS)
public func sendQrCodes(_ data: [String: Any]) {
  // 1
  let key = ConnectivityUserInfoKey.qrCodes.rawValue
  guard let ids = data[key] as? [Int], !ids.isEmpty else
{ return }

  let tempDir = FileManager.default.temporaryDirectory

  // 2
  TicketOffice.shared
    .movies
    .filter { ids.contains($0.id) }
    .forEach { movie in
      // 3
      let image = QRCode.generate(
        movie: movie,
        size: .init(width: 100, height: 100)
      )

      // 4
      guard let data = image?.pngData() else { return }

      // 5
      let url =
tempDir.appendingPathComponent(UUID().uuidString)
      guard let _ = try? data.write(to: url) else {
        return
      }

      // 6
      WCSession.default.transferFile(url, metadata: [key:
movie.id])
```

```
    }
  }
  #endif
```

Here's a code breakdown:

1. If the data passed to the method doesn't contain a list of movie IDs that require a QR code, then exit the method.
2. Grab all of the movies which exist with the requested IDs. Silently ignore bad IDs.
3. Now that you have an actual `Movie` object, generate a QR code for it at a size that will work well on the Apple Watch.
4. If either the QR code failed to generate an image or the image couldn't generate PNG data, there's nothing more to do here. So, move on to the next one.
5. Generate a temporary file with a unique name and write the PNG data to that file. If it fails, quietly return.
6. Finally, initiate a file transfer to the peer device, meaning the Apple Watch.

Notice how `metadata` contains the ID of the movie whose QR code you just generated.

Call that method first in `update(from:)`:

```
#if os(iOS)
sendQrCodes(dictionary)
#endif
```

It's important to do so *before* the rest of the code because you might have been asked for a QR code again and had no new purchases.

Of course, it wouldn't be connectivity code if you didn't have to implement another delegate! Add the following method to the delegate section:

```
// 1
#if os(watchOS)
func session(_ session: WCSession, didReceive file:
WCSessionFile) {
  // 2
  let key = ConnectivityUserInfoKey.qrCodes.rawValue
  guard let id = file.metadata?[key] as? Int else {
    return
  }

  // 3
```

```
    let destination = QRCode.url(for: id)

    // 4
    try? FileManager.default.removeItem(at: destination)
    try? FileManager.default.moveItem(at: file.fileURL, to:
destination)
}
#endif
```

In the preceding code, you:

1. Only receive a file transfer on watchOS, so you wrap it in a compiler check.
2. Pull the movie's ID from the metadata. If no ID exists, quietly exit the method.
3. Determine where you should write the indicated movie's QR code.
4. Remove the QR code if there's already one there, and then move the received file to the proper location.

> **Note**: watchOS will delete the received file if it still exists when the method ends. You must *synchronously* move the file to a new location if you wish to keep it.

Now that you have a way to request and receive QR codes, you just need to modify the `TicketOffice` code. Open **Shared/TicketOffice** and edit the `delete` method. If you delete a ticket from the Apple Watch, you might as well remove the image, too. At the start of the method, add:

```
#if os(watchOS)
offsets
  .map { purchased[$0].id }
  .forEach { id in
    let url = QRCode.url(for: id)
    try? FileManager.default.removeItem(at: url)
  }
#endif
```

Here, you map each row you delete to the corresponding movie's ID. Once you have a list of IDs, you determine where the QR code is stored and then remove it.

Now edit `updateCompanion` to figure out which movies still need a QR code. Replace the existing connectivity call with:

```
// 1
var wantedQrCodes: [Int] = []

// 2
#if os(watchOS)
wantedQrCodes = ids.filter { id in
  let url = QRCode.url(for: id)
  return !FileManager.default.fileExists(atPath: url.path)
}
#endif

// 3
Connectivity.shared.send(
  movieIds: ids,
  delivery: .highPriority,
  wantedQrCodes: wantedQrCodes
)
```

You add a few minor updates here:

1. You store a list of all QR codes you need to request, defaulting to none.
2. If running on the Apple Watch, you identify all purchased movies that don't have a stored QR code yet.
3. Finally, you include `wantedQrCodes` in the connectivity call.

Next, you'll add some code to the end of the `Movie` struct to retrieve the locally stored QR code. Open **Shared/Movie** and add the following:

```
#if os(watchOS)
func qrCodeImage() -> Image? {
  let path = QRCode.url(for: id).path
  if let image = UIImage(contentsOfFile: path) {
    return Image(uiImage: image)
  } else {
    return Image(systemName: "xmark.circle")
  }
}
#endif
```

If the QR code exists where it's supposed to, you return it as a SwiftUI `Image`. If the image doesn't exist, then you return an appropriate default image instead.

Finally, you need to check for the movie purchase. Open **CinemaTime Watch App/MovieDetailsView** and add `else` like this:

```
if !ticketOffice.isPurchased(movie) {
  PurchaseTicketView(movie: movie)
} else {
  movie.qrCodeImage()
}
```

Build and rerun your app. Purchase a movie from the Apple Watch. After some time, you'll see the QR code at the bottom of the details screen if you navigate away from and back to the details view.

Key Points

- There are many methods available for sending data. Be sure you choose one based on how quickly you need the data to arrive.
- If you send an interactive message from your watchOS app, the corresponding iOS app will wake up in the background and become reachable.
- If you send an interactive message from your iOS app while the watchOS app is *not* in the foreground, the message will fail.
- Bundle messages together whenever possible to limit battery consumption.
- Do not supply a reply handler if you aren't going to reply.

Where to Go From Here?

In this chapter, you set up the Watch Connectivity framework, learned about the different ways to transfer data between counterpart iOS and watchOS apps, and successfully implemented the application context transfer method.

Keeping your iOS and watchOS apps in sync through data transfer is important. That way, users can use both devices indistinctly. In the next chapter, you will learn how to provide users a quick view of the current state of your app. By using Snapshots, you produce apps that feel responsive and up to date.

Chapter 5: Snapshots

By Scott Grosch

The Dock on the Apple Watch lets the wearer see either the recently run apps or their favorite apps. Since watchOS already displays your app at the appropriate time, why should you care about the Dock?

While watchOS will insert an image of your app into the Dock, it'll only display whatever the current screen contains, which may not be the best user experience.

In this chapter, you'll build **UHL**, the official app for the Underwater Hockey League. You may not have heard of this sport before, and you're not alone. Underwater hockey has a cult following. Two teams maneuver a puck across the bottom of a swimming pool.

You're probably feeling the urge to dive in, so time to get to it. CANNONBALL!

Getting Started

Open **UHL.xcodeproj** from the starter folder. Build and run the **UHL Watch App** scheme.

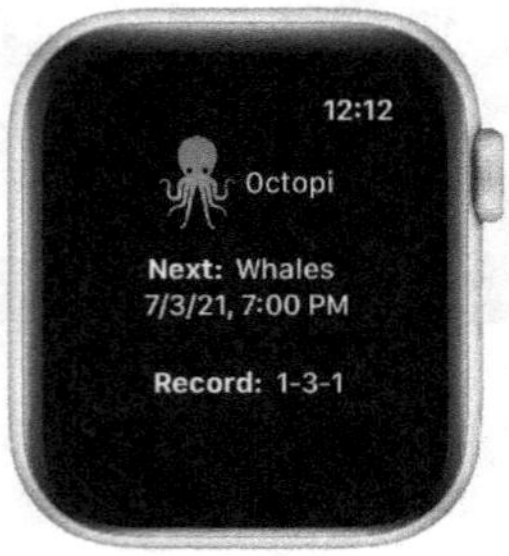

With the UHL app, you can track the best team in the league: Octopi. Take a moment to explore the app. You'll see Octopi's record as well as the details of what matches are coming up next.

The Dock

The Apple Watch has only two physical buttons. While the Digital Crown is the most visible, there's also a Side button right below the crown. Most users interact with the Side button by quickly pressing it twice to bring up Apple Pay.

If you press the button a single time, the Dock will launch. The Dock displays one of two sets of apps:

1. Recently run
2. Favorites

By default, recently run apps will display in the Dock:

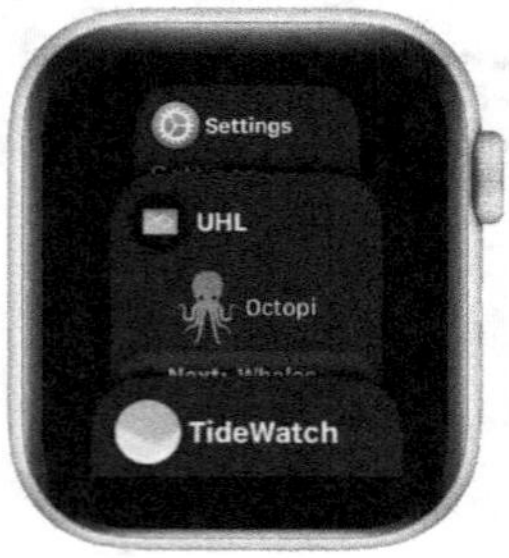

> **Note**: If you choose favorites, then you'll *only* see apps that you've identified. The most recently run app no longer displays in the Dock. To choose what appears, you have to open the Watch app on your iPhone, tap **My Watch**, then tap **Dock** and select either **Recents** or **Favorites**.

The Dock provides multiple benefits:

- Tapping an image launches the app *immediately*.
- Quickly switching between apps.
- Showing current app status at a glance.
- App organization.

Apps currently in the Dock have an almost immediate launch time, as they're kept in memory. In this chapter, your focus is the third bullet. Apps in the Dock show a screenshot of the app's current state called a **snapshot**.

To see an example of snapshots in action, grab your Apple Watch and start a timer. You'll need a **physical device** as the simulator doesn't provide timers.

Once the timer is running, press the **Side button** and scroll to the Timer. It *appears* to be counting down in the Dock, but in reality, that's not what's happening.

The Dock is nothing more than a *static image* of the current state of the app. There are no interactive controls in the Dock. If you tap the snapshot, the app will launch. The Timer app *appears* to be updating as the app has configured itself to take a new snapshot every second.

Snapshot API

By default, when the Dock appears, the user sees what each app looked like before moving to the background. For most apps, nothing more is necessary. Sometimes, such as in the case of the Timer app, a single snapshot is not enough.

You, as the developer, are responsible for telling watchOS if it needs to perform extra snapshots once the app moves to the background. Before diving into the code, you should keep some rules of thumb in mind.

Snapshot Tips

Next, we are going to learn some **tips and tricks** you should take into account if you want to optimize your app snapshots.

Optimizing for Miniaturization

The snapshot is a scaled-down image of your app's full-size dimensions. Be sure to carefully look at all the screens which you capture in a snapshot. Is the text still readable? Do images make sense at a smaller size?

Remember:

- At smaller sizes, bolder fonts are easier to read. You may wish to use bolded fonts or larger font sizes for important information.
- You may also need to consider removing less important elements from the screen.

Customizing the Interface

Recall that the snapshot is just an image of the app's current display. With that in mind, you could make a custom `View` for when watchOS takes a snapshot and *completely redesign the UI*. **Don't do that**.

Having a custom view could make sense in some situations, especially if you need to remove some elements from the snapshot. If you make a custom view, you want to ensure that the snapshot doesn't look radically different from the normal display. People expect the snapshot to represent your app. If the snapshot looks too different, it becomes hard to recognize and find the app they're looking for.

If you determine that you do need a different visual, please keep these points in mind:

1. Focus on important information.
2. Hide objects that aren't as relevant when viewed in the Dock.
3. Exaggerate the size of certain objects for legibility.
4. Don't make the interface look radically different.

Progress and Status

Progress screens, timers and general status updates are great use cases for snapshots. You may think that complications cover all of those cases. Hopefully, you created said complications! However, you need to remember that your customers may not want to use your complication.

During the COVID-19 pandemic, food delivery services became a major business. Online ordering apps are a perfect example of custom snapshots.

When you order the food, you see one view. Once the restaurant receives your order, the screen could change to show how long until the food is ready for pickup. When the driver gets the food, the screen could show how long until delivery.

During state changes, be sure that you're not snapshotting errors or confirmation dialogs. Such issues are better handled via a local notification.

Changing Screens

Keep the currently active view the same as when the user last interacted with your app whenever possible. If the app's state changes in unpredictable ways, it can confuse and disorient the user. You want the interaction between the Dock and your app to be so seamless that your customers don't understand anything special is happening. If you need to leave the app in a different state, ensure that the end-user can quickly determine what happened.

> **Note**: In the interests of keeping the sample app less complicated, UHL blatantly violates this tip. :]

Anticipating a Timeline

The inverse to the previous tip is that you should anticipate what the user would want to see when they look in the Dock.

Similar to the food delivery example, consider a sporting event. Depending on the time of the event, you might want to have something like this:

- Shortly before the game, users want to see the time and location.
- During the game, users want to see the current score.
- After the game, users want to see the final score and your team's record.
- Other times, users likely want to see the season's schedule.

User Preferences

Not every user is going to want to see the same thing. Can your app offer the possibility of customizing views even further?

A fair-weather fan who only cares about a single team will need a different experience than a sports fanatic who wants to follow the entire league. The fair-weather fan would probably expect the last game's score to stick around in a snapshot much longer than the fanatic who constantly keeps up-to-date.

When Snapshots Happen

watchOS automatically schedules snapshots to update on your behalf in many different scenarios:

- When the Apple Watch boots up.
- When a complication update occurs.
- When the app transitions from the foreground to the background.
- When the user views a long look notification.
- One hour after the user last interacted with the app.
- At least once an hour for apps in the Dock. The Dock takes one snapshot every six minutes rotating through each app in sequence. If the user has fewer than ten apps in the Dock, each app will receive more frequent snapshot tasks than one per hour.
- At optional, scheduled times, with the Background Refresh API.

Working With Snapshots

Now that you better understand how to use snapshots, it's time to implement what you've learned in the UHL app!

> **Note**: The simulator frequently gets confused while working with snapshots and the Dock. If that happens, quit and restart the simulator or preferably use a physical device instead.

Snapshots Handler

First, you need to implement the method watchOS calls when it's time to take snapshot. Open **ExtensionDelegate** and add the following method:

```
func handle(_ backgroundTasks: Set<WKRefreshBackgroundTask>) {
  // 1
  backgroundTasks.forEach { task in
    // 2
    guard let snapshot = task as?
WKSnapshotRefreshBackgroundTask else {
      task.setTaskCompletedWithSnapshot(false)
      return
    }

    // 3
    print("Taking a snapshot")

    // 4
    task.setTaskCompletedWithSnapshot(true)
  }
}
```

Whenever watchOS wakes up your app from the background, it calls `handle(_:)`. Here's what the preceding code accomplishes:

1. First, it schedules one or more tasks for you to handle. Loop through each one.
2. You only care about snapshots, so mark the task completed if it's not a snapshot. Passing `false` tells the system not to auto-schedule another snapshot.
3. I'll bet this statement confuses you! :]
4. Finally, you mark the snapshot task as complete and specify `true` so that watchOS automatically schedules another snapshot for an hour from now.

When watchOS calls `handle(_:)`, you have a limited amount of time, on the order of seconds, to finish the task. If you neglect to mark the task as having completed, the system continues to run it in the background. Your task will then run until all available time has been consumed, which wastes battery power.

In step two, where you pass `false` to `setTaskCompletedWithSnapshot`, you might be wondering why you don't specify `true` instead. Since you took no action on the task, there's no reason to force an immediate snapshot to happen.

Bring up Xcode's Debug area by pressing **Shift-Command-C**. Then build and run your app.

Once the simulator is running your app, switch to the Home screen. Be patient — after an indeterminate, but likely short, amount of time, you'll see the message that your app took a snapshot.

Forcing a Snapshot

When you switched to the Home screen, the snapshot task didn't immediately run because watchOS was busy performing other tasks. That might be OK for a normal production deployment, but when building the app, you'll want to be able to tell the simulator to take a snapshot *right now*.

Remember that snapshots will only occur if the app is *not* in the foreground. The simulator — or physical device — must be showing any other app or the clock face. Of course, the app must be running via Xcode for you to see the fruits of your labor.

Once your app is running in the background, in *Xcode*'s menu bar, choose **Debug ▸ Simulate UI Snapshot**.

You might think you'd use the simulator to force a snapshot in it. Unfortunately, you'd be wrong. It's easy to get confused and wonder why you can't find the **Simulate UI Snapshot** menu bar item.

You'll see the message in the Debug area again, letting you know watchOS took a snapshot. Notice how nothing else on the watch face changes. Snapshots are a background task, meaning there's no reason for watchOS to bring your app to the user's attention.

Viewing a Snapshot

You can see what your snapshot looks like by visiting the Dock. In the simulator, you get to the Dock in three separate ways:

1. Click the Side button in the simulated Apple Watch display.
2. Click **Device ▸ Side Button** in the simulator's menu bar.
3. Press **Shift-Command-B** on your keyboard. Scholars have pondered for ages why it's not **Shift-Command-D**. :]

After bringing up the dock, you'll see that your app is the first on the list:

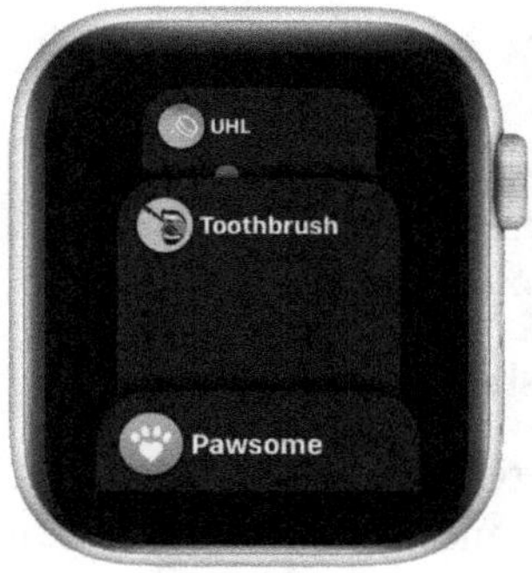

That doesn't give you a great view of your snapshot, though. Run any other app, and then jump back to the dock. Now, you'll have a better view of your snapshot:

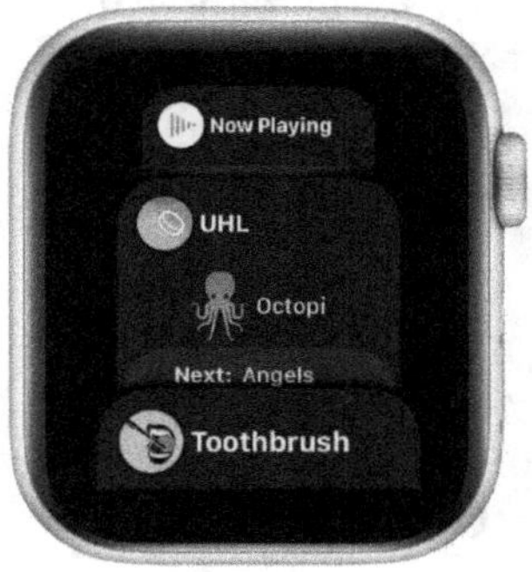

Customizing the Snapshot

As previously discussed, your app's snapshot defaults to the last screen which was visible. That's not helpful for Octopi fans.

If the last match played occurred yesterday or today, you should show them the score of that match. If, instead, the next match will occur today or tomorrow, show that match's schedule. Otherwise, take a new snapshot two days later.

Add the following method to `ExtensionDelegate`:

```
private func nextSnapshotDate() -> Date {
  // 1
  guard let nextMatch = Season.shared.nextMatch else {
    return .distantFuture
  }

  // 2
  let twoDaysLater = Calendar.current.date(
```

```
    byAdding: .day,
    value: 2,
    to: nextMatch.date
  )!

  // 3
  return Calendar.current.startOfDay(for: twoDaysLater)
}
```

The preceding code accomplishes these three tasks:

1. If there's no upcoming match, you return `.distantFuture` for the date. Using `.distantFuture` essentially tells watchOS that there are no more scheduled snapshots.
2. Using calendrical calculations, you determine what the date will be in two days. This calculation can't fail, so it's safe to force unwrap the return value.
3. Finally, you determine the start of the day for when the snapshot will happen.

Snapshot User Info

The Snapshot API is based around a user info type dictionary. While you *could* use a dictionary, there's a better way to handle the data. You don't want to have to hardcode strings for the keys or define global `let` type constants. Instead, create a new Swift file named **SnapshotUserInfo**.

When a snapshot happens, you have to switch the app to the appropriate screen depending on the rules previously defined. The sample app already has much of the code implemented to handle that task for you. The goal here is to learn about snapshots, not the craziness that is controlling which SwiftUI view gets automatically pushed onto the navigation stack.

Start with:

```
import Foundation

struct SnapshotUserInfo {
  // 1
  let handler: () -> Void
  // 2
  let destination: ContentView.Destination
  // 3
  let matchId: Match.ID?
}
```

`SnapshotUserInfo` implemented this so far:

1. You have to tell the snapshot when it's completed. More on that in a moment.
2. `ContentView.Destination` is an `enum` identifying which view will be pushed onto the navigation stack.
3. You need to identify a match to snapshot.

Look in **Match** located in **Model** group. You'll see that the `Identifiable` protocol is implemented, and the type of the identifier is a `UUID`. While you could use a `UUID` type throughout the app, it's a better idea to reference `Match.ID` instead. Why? If at a later date you realize you need the identifier to be an `Int` instead, there's only a single location you need to update.

Next, in **SnapshotUserInfo**, implement an initializer:

```
init(
  handler: @escaping () -> Void,
  destination: ContentView.Destination,
  matchId: Match.ID? = nil
) {
  self.handler = handler
  self.destination = destination
  self.matchId = matchId
}
```

While not technically required, implementing the initializer lets you initialize the structure instance without having to explicitly specify `nil` for the match.

Now you need a way to generate the dictionary that the Snapshot API wants. Add:

```
// 1
private enum Keys: String {
  case handler, destination, matchId
}

// 2
func encode() -> [AnyHashable: Any] {
  return [
    Keys.handler.rawValue: handler,
    Keys.destination.rawValue: destination,
    // 3
    Keys.matchId.rawValue: matchId as Any
  ]
}
```

Here's a code breakdown:

1. You define an `enum` to store the keys to the dictionary. You could also use `let` strings, but the `enum` is cleaner for this use case.
2. You create a method that encodes the `struct` into the type of dictionary the Snapshot API requires.
3. The match identifier could be `nil`, so you must explicitly add the `as Any` cast to make the compiler happy.

You'll also need a way to convert from the API's dictionary into the object you defined. Add a custom error type right outside the `struct`:

```
enum SnapshotError: Error {
  case noHandler, badDestination, badMatchId, noUserInfo
}
```

Then inside the `struct`, implement the method to convert from the API's dictionary information:

```
// 1
static func from(notification: Notification) throws -> Self {
  // 2
  guard let userInfo = notification.userInfo else {
    throw SnapshotError.noUserInfo
  }

  guard let handler = userInfo[Keys.handler.rawValue] as? () ->
Void else {
    throw SnapshotError.noHandler
  }

  guard
    let destination = userInfo[Keys.destination.rawValue] as?
ContentView.Destination
  else {
    throw SnapshotError.badDestination
  }

  // 3
  return .init(
    handler: handler,
    destination: destination,
    // 4
    matchId: userInfo[Keys.matchId.rawValue] as? Match.ID
  )
}
```

Here's what's happening:

1. Using a `static` method allows for a factory pattern type of creation.
2. You pull the individual pieces out of the posted `Notification`, throwing an appropriate error if anything goes wrong.
3. Then, you create and return a properly initialized object.
4. Similarly to the other method, using an `as? Match.ID` cast handles the case when no match identifier is provided.

Viewing the Last Game's Score

Sometimes, even the best of fans will miss a game. If the most recent match was yesterday or today, wouldn't it be great if you showed the score?

In **Season**, inside the **Model** group, find the following line of code:

```
bySettingHour: Int.random(in: 18 ... 20),
```

Update the values to be something earlier in the day than the current hour. You want to make it appear like a match already happened today.

Add the following method to the **ExtensionDelegate** class:

```
private func lastMatchPlayedRecently() -> Bool {
  // 1
  guard let last = Season.shared.pastMatches().last?.date else {
    return false
  }

  // 2
  return Calendar.current.isDateInYesterday(last) ||
         Calendar.current.isDateInToday(last)
}
```

Here's what's happening:

1. If there's a previously played match, grab the date. If not, simply return `false`.
2. Determine if the last match occurred yesterday or today.

In the `handle(_:)` method, delete the final line which completes the snapshot and replace it with:

```
let nextSnapshotDate = nextSnapshotDate()

let handler = {
  snapshot.setTaskCompleted(
    restoredDefaultState: false,
    estimatedSnapshotExpiration: nextSnapshotDate,
    userInfo: nil
  )
}
```

`setTaskCompletedWithSnapshot(_:)` is a convenience method for the longer `setTaskCompleted(restoredDefaultState:estimatedSnapshotExpiration:userInfo)`. Try saying that one three times fast!

- When watchOS takes the snapshot, you tell it to complete the task. You pass `false` to the first parameter because you left the app in a different state than it was originally in.
- The second parameter, `estimatedSnapshotExpiration`, tells watchOS when the current snapshot is no longer valid. Essentially, the date you provide is when it needs to take a new snapshot.
- Finally, for the `userInfo` parameter, simply pass `nil` as you don't need the next snapshot to know anything about the app's current state. If you did, `userInfo` is where you could pass something along.

Notice how you've assigned that completion call to a `handler` variable. You don't want to *complete* the task until you're ready for watchOS to take the snapshot, which means you first have to get the views pushed onto the navigation stack. That's why your `SnapshotUserInfo` has a `handler` property.

Continue adding to `handle(_:)`:

```
// 1
var snapshotUserInfo: SnapshotUserInfo?

// 2
if lastMatchPlayedRecently() {
  snapshotUserInfo = SnapshotUserInfo(
    handler: handler,
    destination: .record
  )
}

// 3
if let snapshotUserInfo = snapshotUserInfo {
  NotificationCenter.default.post(
    name: .pushViewForSnapshot,
    object: nil,
    userInfo: snapshotUserInfo.encode()
  )
} else {
  // 4
  handler()
}
```

Lots going on with that code:

1. You create a variable of type `SnapshotUserInfo`, which is currently not set.
2. If there's been a recent match, you populate that variable with the `handler` you just defined and specify that the record view is what should display in the snapshot.
3. If there's data for the `snapshotUserInfo`, you post a notification with that object. Notice how the `userInfo` of the notification is the encoded object.
4. If not, then you simply call the handler to complete the task.

The sample project includes a file called **Notification.Name+Extension** which defines the notification type for you.

Putting the details into a `struct` instead of just populating the `userInfo` dictionary directly makes the code much cleaner. By abstracting away the data's details, it also becomes much easier to test.

Phew! That's quite a bit of code. Press **Command-B** to do a quick build of your project to make sure you haven't missed anything. It'll compile cleanly with neither warnings nor errors at this point.

When the system wants to take a snapshot, and there's a recently played match, you now post a notification with the details. When the notification happens, the app needs to navigate to `RecordView`.

Edit **RecordView**, located in **Record**, then add a new property to the `RecordView` structure:

```
let snapshotHandler: (() -> Void)?
```

Then update the `PreviewProvider` appropriately:

```
RecordView(snapshotHandler: nil)
```

Remember that the handler you created in `ExtensionDelegate` needs to be called when the snapshot is ready to be taken.

When `RecordView` is the active view, then, and only then, can you complete the background task. watchOS 8 added a wonderful new `View` method called `task`, which is perfect for your needs. The code in the `task` block will run one time when the view appears and will cancel when the view goes away.

Add a call to the snapshot handler to the `List` view:

```
var body: some View {
  List(season.pastMatches().reversed()) {
    ...
  }
  ...
  .task {
    snapshotHandler?()
  }
}
```

Once the view appears, if `snapshotHandler` has a value, the method will be called, appropriately signifying to the snapshot task that it is complete.

Finally, edit **ContentView** and add two new properties:

```
// 1
@State private var snapshotHandler: (() -> Void)?

// 2
private let pushViewForSnapshotPublisher = NotificationCenter
  .default
  .publisher(for: .pushViewForSnapshot)
```

For those two properties:

1. Since `ContentView` is the top of your navigation stack, the property you store the snapshot handler in has to be `@State` as this is the view that will assign the value based on the notification.
2. Taking advantage of Combine makes responding to notifications quite simple in SwiftUI.

Add a function to call the snapshot handler and then clear it out so it doesn't get called a second time.

```
private func handleSnapshot() {
  snapshotHandler?()
  snapshotHandler = nil
}
```

Now you can fix the compiler error by passing the function call to the `RecordView` initializer:

```
RecordView(snapshotHandler: handleSnapshot)
```

Next, add a new method to handle when the notification is called:

```
private func pushViewForSnapshot(_ notification: Notification) {
  // 1
  guard let info = try? SnapshotUserInfo.from(notification:
notification) else {
    return
  }

  // 2
  snapshotHandler = info.handler

  // 3
  path.append(info.destination)

  // 4
  if let matchId = info.matchId, let match = season.match(with:
matchId) {
    path.append(.matchDetail(match: match))
  }
}
```

For `pushViewForSnapshot(_:)`:

1. You pull the `SnapshotUserInfo` details from the notification you posted in `ExtensionDelegate`.
2. Extract the handler into a local variable for ease of use.
3. Adding the destination to `path` is what tells the UI to switch to that particular view.
4. If the info provides a specific match, add a detail view for that match to the navigation path.

> **Note**: When the user taps on an app in the doc, the app will still have the state from the last snapshot. Adding more than one destination to the navigation path puts the navigation path in the same state it would be in if the user tapped through to the match detail view themselves.

All that's left to do is "catch" the notification. After the second `NavigationLink`, before closing the `VStack`, call your helper method when a notification appears:

```
.onReceive(pushViewForSnapshotPublisher) {
  pushViewForSnapshot($0)
}
```

Note: There are multiple ways to catch and handle a notification in SwiftUI. Use whatever method feels most natural to you.

At this point, build and run the app. Perform the following steps to test all your hard work:

1. Ensure you've navigated to the first screen of the app.
2. Change to the Home screen.
3. In Xcode's menu bar, click **Debug ▸ Simulate UI Snapshot**.
4. In the simulator, bring up the Dock.

You'll now see that your app did move to the proper view before taking a snapshot.

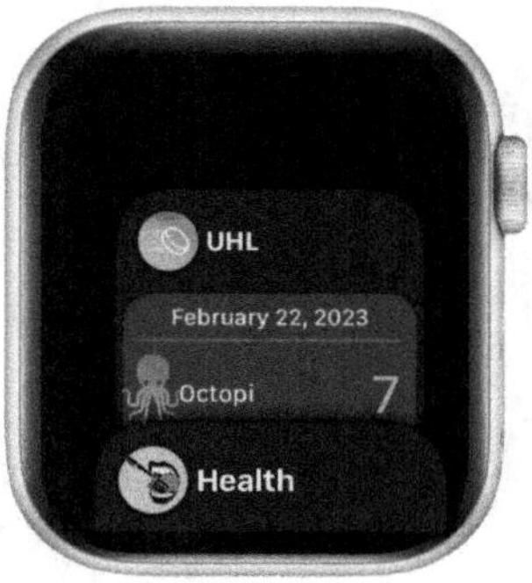

Wow, that was a ton of code! Take a quick break if you need to, and then it'll be time to handle upcoming matches.

Viewing Upcoming Matches

If there's no recent match, there might be a pending one. Edit **ExtensionDelegate** and add another method:

```
private func idForPendingMatch() -> Match.ID? {
  guard let match = Season.shared.nextMatch else {
    return nil
  }

  let date = match.date
  let calendar = Calendar.current

  if calendar.isDateInTomorrow(date) ||
calendar.isDateInToday(date) {
    return match.id
  } else {
    return nil
  }
}
```

The code is pretty self-explanatory. If there's a match today or tomorrow, return the match's identifier. Otherwise, return `nil`.

In the `handle(_:)` method, find the `if`, where you check for a recently played match:

```
if lastMatchPlayedRecently() {
  snapshotUserInfo = SnapshotUserInfo(
    handler: handler,
    destination: .record
  )
}
```

And add `else` branch with print statements, so it'll take the following form:

```
if lastMatchPlayedRecently() {
  print("Going to record")
  snapshotUserInfo = SnapshotUserInfo(
    handler: handler,
    destination: .record
  )
} else if let id = idForPendingMatch() {
  print("Going to schedule")
  snapshotUserInfo = SnapshotUserInfo(
    handler: handler,
    destination: .schedule,
    matchId: id
  )
}
```

When the notification happens, the app needs to navigate to `ScheduleView` and then `ScheduleDetailView` for the specified `matchId`. That's a bit complicated in SwiftUI, but the code is already there for you. You just need to add in the snapshot specific details now.

Working backward, to help avoid compiler errors while you're coding, first edit **ScheduleDetailView**. You'll perform similar steps to what you did for the record view. Add a new property:

```
let snapshotHandler: (() -> Void)?
```

Then calls the snapshot handler in a `.task`:

```
VStack {
  ...
  VStack {
    ...
  }
}
.task {
  snapshotHandler?()
}
```

And update the `PreviewProvider`:

```
ScheduleDetailView(
  match: Season.shared.nextMatch!,
  snapshotHandler: nil
)
```

Make the same changes to **ScheduleView**, remembering all three steps:

1. Add the `snapshotHandler` property.
2. Add the `.task` to the end of the `body`.
3. Update the `PreviewProvider` to pass in a `nil` value for the `snapshotHandler`.

In your best pirate voice, think, "Here be compiler errors."

Back in **ContentView**, inside the `navigationDestination(for:)` modifier, update the call to include the snapshot provider:

```
.navigationDestination(for: Destination.self) { destination in
  switch destination {
  case .schedule:
    ScheduleView(snapshotHandler: handleSnapshot)
  case .record:
    RecordView(snapshotHandler: handleSnapshot)
  case .matchDetail(let match):
    ScheduleDetailView(match: match, snapshotHandler:
handleSnapshot)
  }
}
```

Build and run the app. This time, tap the first button to navigate to the upcoming matches view. Swipe left on a row, and you'll see a button to add a match as well as delete the current match:

Tap the + button to create a random match that occurs today. Also, the most recent match which occurred earlier today or yesterday is removed to ensure that the record view doesn't appear.

Force another snapshot as you did for the record view:

1. Ensure you've navigated to the first screen of the app.
2. Change to the Home screen.
3. In Xcode's menu bar, click **Debug ▸ Simulate UI Snapshot**.
4. In the simulator, bring up the Dock.

You'll see that you now display the schedule view in the Dock:

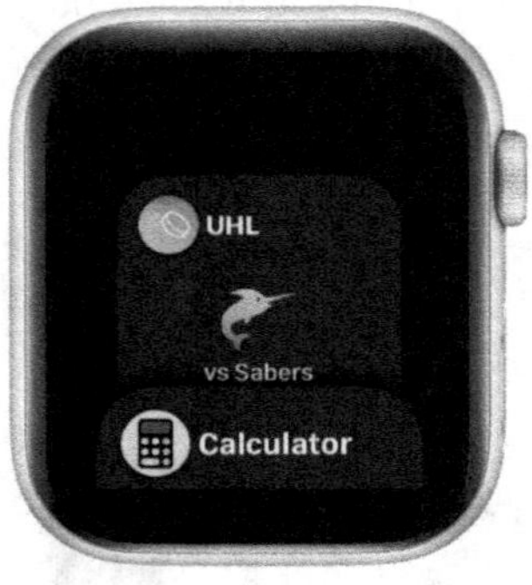

Key Points

- Make sure you always mark background tasks as completed as soon as possible. If you don't, you'll waste the user's battery.
- Snapshots are smaller than your app. Consider bolding text, removing images or making other minor changes to increase the information displayed.

Where to Go From Here?

The chapter's sample code includes a **ModifiedRecordView.swift** file (in the same directory as **starter** and **final**), which shows an example of how you might detect that a snapshot is about to happen so that you can present a different view entirely if that makes sense for your app.

Now you're a Dock connoisseur, and you've gained a deep understanding of how watchOS uses snapshots. You also learned how to modify snapshots based on contextual relevance.

If you'd like to take this further, try tweaking the size or color of objects in the snapshot. Remember that the snapshot is miniaturized, so you might want to make the text more readable.

Chapter 6: Notifications

By Scott Grosch

Local and remote notifications are a great way to inform your users about new or relevant information. There may be new content available, it might be their turn in the game or they may have just won the lottery. If your app has an accompanying iPhone app that supports notifications, by default, your Apple Watch will display the notification when appropriate. However, you can do better!

Where Did It Go?

Apple tries to determine the best target device to receive a notification. If you only have an Apple Watch, it'll go there. However, if you use a watch and another device, the destination depends not only on the type of notification but also on its source.

The diagram below will help you understand how Apple chooses which device should display the notification. As you can see, the notification type, whether it is Local, Remote or a Background notification, will define where it should go. For the first two options, local and background, it will prioritize the Apple Watch. Local Notifications on the other hand will prioritize depending on the source. Check the following image to see the different paths:

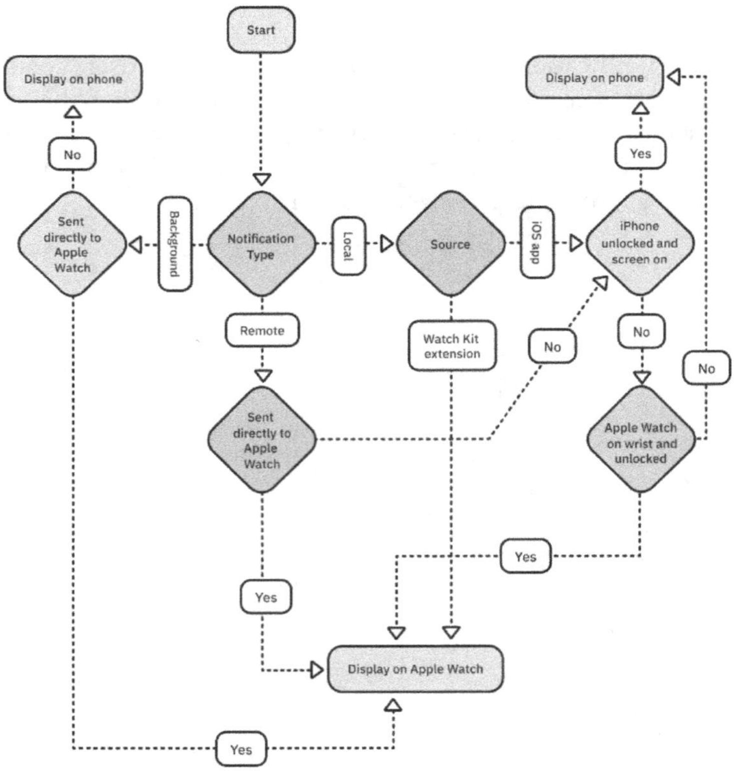

You'll notice two locations in the diagram where it asks if Apple sent the notification directly to the watch. In watchOS 6 and later, the Apple Watch is a valid target for remote and background notifications. The Apple Watch extension receives a unique device token when registering for remote notifications, just like in iOS.

Short Looks

When the Apple Watch receives a notification, it notifies the user via a subtle vibration. If the user views the notification by raising their wrist, the Apple Watch shows an abbreviated version called a **short look**. If the user views the notification for more than a split second, the Apple Watch will offer a more detailed version, or **long look**.

The short look notification is a quick summary for the user. Short looks show the app's icon and name, as well as the optional notification title, in a predefined layout:

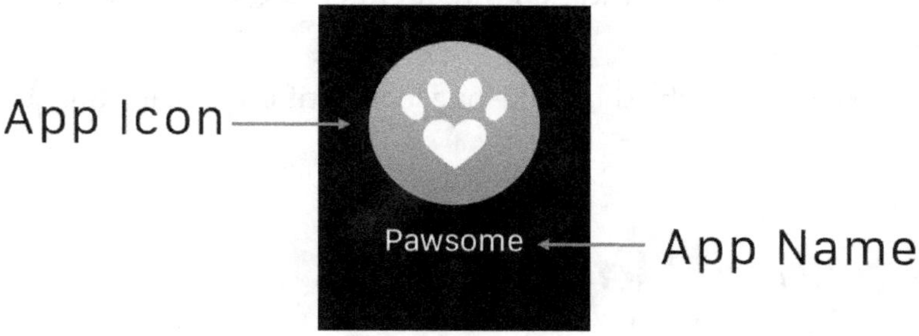

The optional notification title is a short blurb about the notification, such as "New Bill", "Reminder" or "Score Alert", and is added to the `alert` key's value. This lets the user decide whether to stick around for the long look interface.

Long Looks

The long look is a scrolling interface you can customize, with a default static interface or an optional dynamically-created interface. Unlike the short look interface, the long look offers significant customization.

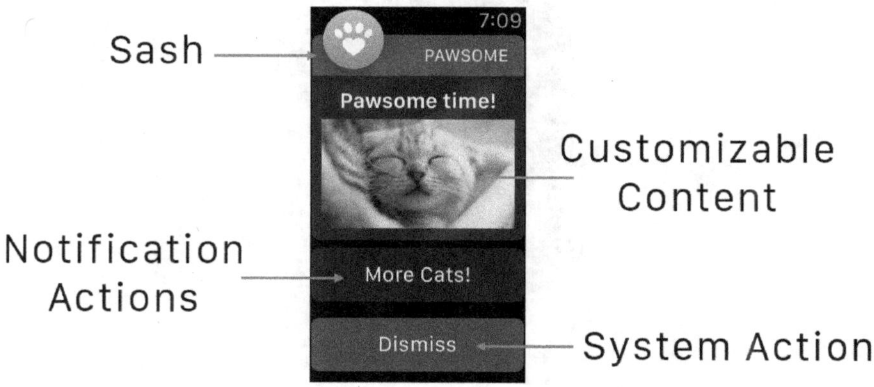

The **sash** is the horizontal bar at the top. It's translucent by default, but you can set it to any color and opacity value.

You can customize the content area by implementing a SwiftUI `View`, which you'll learn about later.

While you can implement several `UNNotificationAction` items, remember that more than a few will require quite a bit of scrolling on the user's part, leading to a poor user experience.

The system-provided Dismiss button is always present at the bottom of the interface. Tapping Dismiss hides the notification without informing the Apple Watch extension.

Now that you know about the short and long look notifications, it's time to put the theory into practice.

Testing Local Notifications

Pawsome is for all cat lovers who procrastinate during the day by looking at cute cat pictures. The Pawsome app will make this easier by interrupting you throughout the day with cute cat pictures that are certain to trigger a smile... unless you're a dog person!

Getting Started

Open the Pawsome starter project in Xcode. Then build and run the **Pawsome WatchKit App** scheme. You'll see a collection of cute kitty cats that you can easily browse:

Testing Notifications With the Simulator

When you create a new Apple Watch app in Xcode, it no longer generates a notification scheme. Click **Product ▸ Scheme ▸ New Scheme...** and name the scheme **Pawsome Notification**:

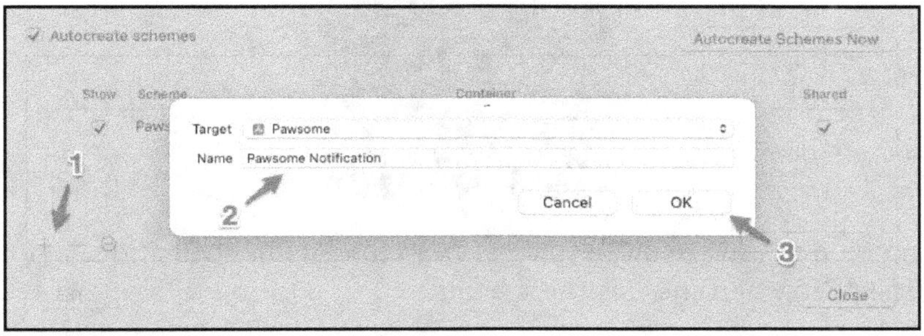

Edit the newly created scheme and make three changes:

1. Set the **Executable** to the watch app.
2. Set the **Watch Interface** to **Dynamic Notification**.
3. Set the **Notification Payload** to **PushNotificationPayload.apns**.

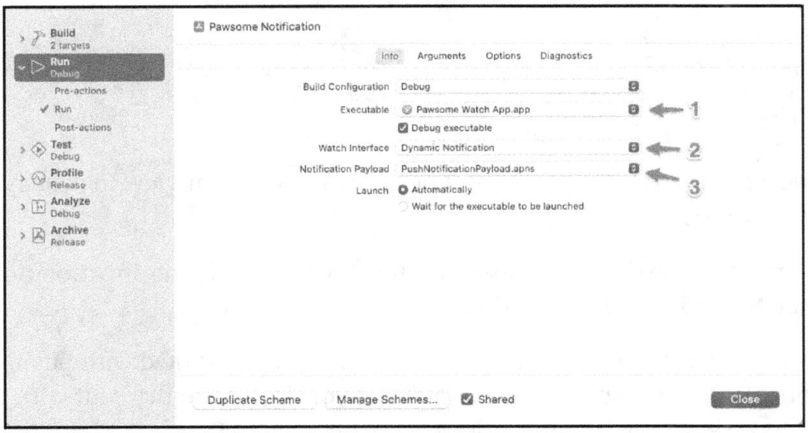

Using the newly created schema, build and run the app, then tap on the notification:

The information of what to display comes from the **PushNotificationPayload** file that you specified when creating the schema.

However, when watchOS delivers an actual notification, you have to specify what SwiftUI View to utilize. Take a look at **LocalNotifications**, and you'll see the code that creates and schedules your local notifications. There's nothing specific to watchOS, which is why I provided that file for you. At the top of the class, you'll find `categoryIdentifier`. When a notification triggers, that's the identifier you'll use.

Open **PawsomeApp**, then add the following to the end of the `body`:

```
WKNotificationScene(
  controller: NotificationController.self,
  category: LocalNotifications.categoryIdentifier
)
```

Calling `WKNotificationScene` is how you tell watchOS what view to display for each category identified in your payload.

Build and run the app. Nothing looks different. Why isn't the notification now using the defined `NotificationController`?

Take a look at **PushNotificationPayload.apns**. If you've worked with push notifications at all, this should look familiar to you. The **category** sent with the notification is set to **myCategory**. However, you updated **PawsomeApp** to respond to a different category name. When the category sent to the app doesn't match something you've registered for, it configures a default display.

Change **myCategory** to **Pawsome**, which is the value of `LocalNotifications.categoryIdentifier`.

Run the app again. This time you'll see:

Where did the "More Cats!" button come from? **PawsomeApp** creates an instance of `LocalNotifications`, which creates a default action button in its initializer.

Since the category in the JSON matches what you specified in `WKNotificationScene(controller:category:)`, watchOS created an instance of `NotificationController` and used that to display the notification. Look closely, and you'll notice the title and body are missing from the displayed view. Time to fix that!

Custom Long Look Notification

Edit **NotificationController**, and you'll see body returns an instance of `NotificationView`. The *controller* is where you receive and parse the notification. The *view* is then where you use the data gathered by the controller.

Switch over to **NotificationView** to make the notification appear the way you want. Replace the entire contents of the default file with:

```
import SwiftUI

struct NotificationView: View {
  // 1
  let message: String
  let image: Image

  // 2
  var body: some View {
    ScrollView {
      Text(message)
        .font(.headline)

      image
        .resizable()
```

```
        .scaledToFit()
    }
  }
}

struct NotificationView_Previews: PreviewProvider {
  static var previews: some View {
    // 3
    NotificationView(
      message: "Awww",
      image: Image("cat\(Int.random(in: 1...20))")
    )
  }
}
```

The code is pretty straight-forward:

1. You need to provide a message and an image for the view to display.
2. The body simply displays those two properties in a scrolling list.
3. For the preview, a random image is chosen from the asset catalog for the previews.

Now that you've created a view to display when a notification arrives, it's time to use it. Head back to **NotificationController** and replace the contents of the class with:

```
// 1
var image: Image!
var message: String!

// 2
override var body: NotificationView {
  return NotificationView(message: message, image: image)
}

// 3
override func didReceive(_ notification: UNNotification) {
  let content = notification.request.content
  message = content.body

  let num = Int.random(in: 1...20)
  image = Image("cat\(num)")
}
```

Like all good code, the controller is short and sweet. It only has a few steps:

1. You store the title and image so you can send them to the view.
2. Then you call the initializer for the view you're going to display, passing in the appropriate parameters.
3. You pull out the details from the payload body, which you then store in the class' properties.

Build and run again, trying to limit the immense feelings of joy caused by the display:

You probably want to display a specific cat, not a random one. Replace the last two lines of `didReceive(_:)` with:

```
let validRange = 1...20
if let imageNumber = content.userInfo["imageNumber"] as? Int,
  validRange ~= imageNumber {
  image = Image("cat\(imageNumber)")
} else {
  let num = Int.random(in: validRange)
  image = Image("cat\(num)")
}
```

The asset catalog provided with the starter project has images numbered from one to twenty. If the payload includes an image number in that range, you display the specified cat photo. If not, you provide a random image.

> **Note**: Since the view will always be generated, you need to ensure that valid data is always available, even if it means presenting a default set of data.

Add the following line right before the final closing } character in **PushNotificationPayload.apns**:

```
, "imageNumber": 19
```

Build and run again. You'll see **cat19** from the asset catalog.

Receiving Remote Push Notifications

Most apps use push notifications, not local notifications. You're probably wondering why I spent all that time on something that's used less frequently. Well, the answer is that Apple made push notifications much easier on watchOS than they are on iOS.

In iOS, you have to create an extension to modify the incoming payload and yet another extension if you want a custom interface. It's also much more difficult to display custom notifications with SwiftUI. In watchOS, push notifications work exactly like local notifications!

Everything you learned about using `WKUserNotificationHostingController` to parse the payload and return a custom SwiftUI `View` works the same when you're developing push notifications.

Create a WKExtensionDelegate

In iOS, you register for push notifications using `AppDelegate`. That class doesn't exist on watchOS. Instead, you use `WKExtensionDelegate`. Create a new Swift file called **ExtensionDelegate** and paste:

```
import WatchKit
import UserNotifications
```

```
// 1
final class ExtensionDelegate: NSObject, WKExtensionDelegate {
  // 2
  func didRegisterForRemoteNotifications(withDeviceToken
deviceToken: Data) {
    print(deviceToken.reduce("") { $0 + String(format: "%02x",
$1) })
  }

  // 3
  func applicationDidFinishLaunching() {
    Task {
      let success = try await UNUserNotificationCenter
        .current()
        .requestAuthorization(options: [.badge, .sound, .alert])

      guard success else { return }

      // 4
      await MainActor.run {
        WKExtension.shared().registerForRemoteNotifications()
      }
    }
  }
}
```

Here's a code breakdown:

1. You declare a class that implements `WKExtensionDelegate`. Since that protocol is based on `NSObjectProtocol` you also need to derive from `NSObject`.
2. Just like in iOS, you grab the `deviceToken` whenever registration happens. A production app would, of course, store and use the token, not just print it.
3. Surprisingly not named `extensionDidFinishLaunching`. You do the standard dance in this method to request permission to use push notifications.
4. If permissions are granted, you use the `WKExtension` singleton to register for push notifications, which calls `didRegisterForRemoteNotifications(withDeviceToken:)` if successful.

To tell watchOS it should use your `ExtensionDelegate`, add the following two lines to the top of the `struct` in **PawsomeApp**:

```
@WKExtensionDelegateAdaptor(ExtensionDelegate.self)
private var extensionDelegate
```

The MVC of Push Notifications

Instead of making you copy and paste a ton of code, I've provided a **Remote Notifications** group in the starter project, which contains the relevant files for a push notification.

Generally, you'll want to use some type of model to represent the data that will pass between your `WKUserNotificationHostingController` and `View`. While you could use individual properties, as in the preceding examples for local notifications, it's better to use a real model, such as the one provided in **RemoteNotificationModel**.

Look at **RemoteNotificationView**, and you'll see it's just a simple setup that shows a small number of details by default. If you tap the toggle, it displays more details. Remember, unlike the iPhone, the Apple Watch has limited display space. You'll need to think differently about how you present notification data to the user.

Next, open **RemoteNotificationController**. Even though you're working with a remote push notification, you'll see everything works the same as when you implemented local notifications. Pay special attention to the `guard` statement.

In an ideal world, the payload provided to your app would always be 100% perfect. However, we don't live in an ideal world, so it's important to always validate the input. If anything goes wrong, you *still* have to provide a model for the notification to display. Don't let your app crash because of bad data!

Adding the Capability

Xcode will perform magic if you add the **Push Notifications** capability. In the Project navigator (**Command-1**), select the project name, **Pawsome**. Then select the **Pawsome Watch App** target.

On the **Signing & Capabilities** tab, add the **Push Notifications** capability. If you try to add a capability and nothing seems to show, that generally means you haven't chosen the correct target.

> **Note**: Xcode does not generate a valid identifier for watchOS push notifications!

Years ago, Apple finally automated almost everything around certificate and identifier generation. Unfortunately, for watchOS push notifications, sometimes it doesn't work.

The solution, while annoying to have to deal with, is quite simple. Go into your team's Certificates, Identifiers & Profiles (https://apple.co/31pwmKV) page on the Apple Developer Portal and manually create an identifier for your watchOS app. Use the app identifier **com.yourcompany.Pawsome.watchkitapp** and add Push Notification support.

> **Note**: Replace **yourcompany** in the app identifier with your team's name.

Add a Scheme

Edit the current scheme via your preferred method. I like to press the **Command+<** keyboard shortcut, or you can click on the current scheme and then click **Edit Scheme...**.

Earlier, you created a notification scheme you used to test the local notifications. You'll need another scheme to test the remote notification because the payload is a different file. You could, of course, just change the file on the existing scheme if you wanted to.

> **Note**: If your app supports more than one notification, you can add multiple APNS files and multiple schemes to make it easy to test each one.

Follow these steps to configure a new scheme:

1. With the notification scheme still chosen, press **Duplicate Scheme** at the bottom of the dialog window.
2. Choose a name for the new scheme, such as **Push Notification**.
3. Click **Run** on the left side of the dialog window.
4. Select **RemotePush.apns** as the notification payload to use.

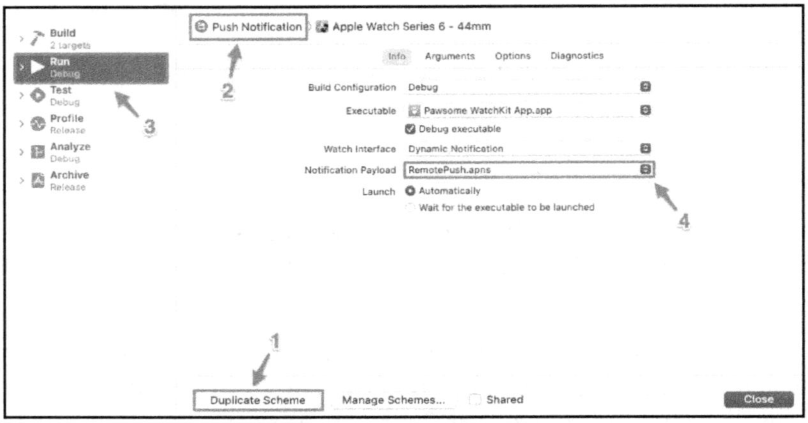

The starter project already includes an .apns file. In your own projects you'll have to add a new one. You'll find **RemotePush.apns** in **Remote Notifications**. It contains a simple example remote push notification payload:

```
{
  "aps": {
    "alert": {
      "body": "Lorem ipsum dolor sit amet, consectetur...",
      "title": "Lorem Ipsum",
    },
    "category": "lorem"
  },

  "date": "2021-04-01T12:00:00Z"
}
```

Remember that watchOS has no way of associating a payload to a controller if you don't link them. Go back into **PawsomeApp** and add the following statement:

```
WKNotificationScene(
  controller: RemoteNotificationController.self,
  category: RemoteNotificationController.categoryIdentifier
)
```

Build and run to take a look at how your remote notification would look on watchOS!

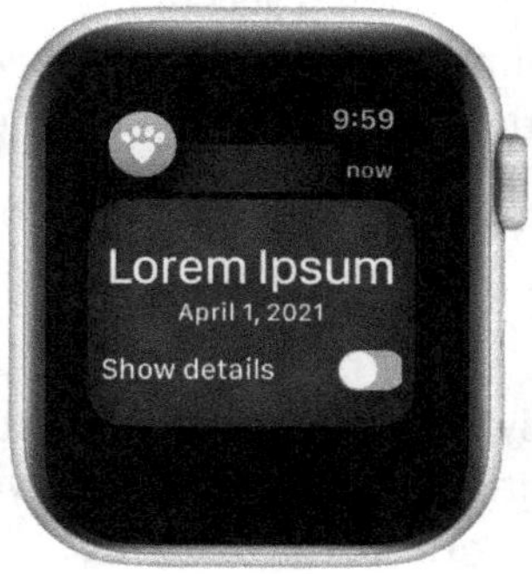

Interactive Notifications

Tap **Show details**. Did something unexpected happen? An average user would expect to see details. Instead, you were taken into the app and shown a cat picture. Surprisingly, that's by design.

By default, push notifications are not interactive. As far as the Apple Watch knows, anything that's not one of the action buttons is just an image on the screen.

Adding an action button wouldn't make sense to show more details. Instead, add the following line to **RemoteNotificationController**:

```
override class var isInteractive: Bool { true }
```

Build and run again. This time, when you tap the toggle, the details appear and disappear as you'd expect them to:

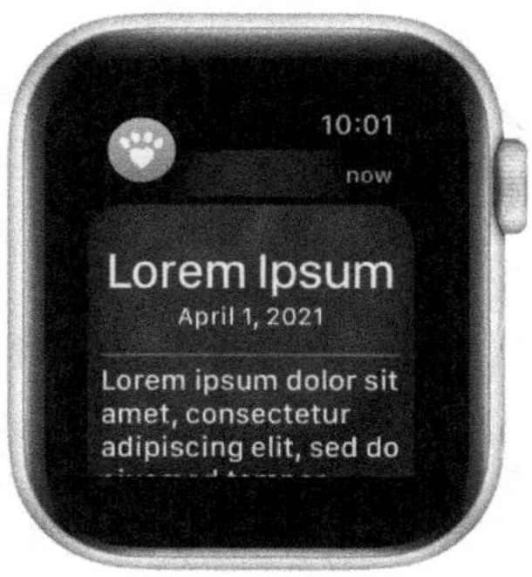

The `isInteractive` type property of `WKUserNotificationHostingController` specifies whether the notification should accept user input. The default value is `false`, meaning you can only interact with buttons. By changing the value to `true`, you tell watchOS the notification should accept user input.

You solved one problem but might have introduced another. Tapping no longer opens the app. If the user taps the app icon or anywhere on the sash, the app will still open.

Great work! Now you know how to add custom notification interfaces to your Watch apps. The rest is up to you! With the power of SwiftUI you are free to put any sort of view on the screen you can imagine, just like on iOS.

APNs Request

A key difference between iOS notifications and watchOS notifications is that you *must* include the **apns-push-type** HTTP header for the Apple Watch to receive a notification.

Apple's Sending Notification Requests to APNs (https://apple.co/3sNr7U4) documents the HTTP headers that you might need to send as part of your POST to APNs.

Key Points

- How Local & Remote Notifications work with Apple Watch.
- Short & Long looks and how to customize them.
- Testing Push Notifications on Apple Watch
- Ensure your server includes the **apns-push-type** HTTP header.

Where to Go From Here?

In this chapter, you tested Watch notifications, learned about short look and long look interfaces and how they differ. Most impressively, you built a custom, dynamically updating, long look local notification for the Apple Watch.

Now you know the basics of showing custom notifications on watchOS, but there's a lot more you can do from here, including handling actions selected by users from your notifications. Please see Apple's User Notifications (https://apple.co/3hFtwKR) documentation as well as our *Push Notifications by Tutorials (*https://bit.ly/3soGsr8*)* book, which is available as part of the professional subscription.

For more details on creating schemes and JSON payloads, as well as testing directly on the watch, please see Testing Custom Notifications (https://apple.co/3tTDE5F) in Apple's developer documentation.

Chapter 7: Lifecycle

By Scott Grosch

The lifecycle of a watchOS app is a bit more complex than that of iOS apps. There are five possible states that a watchOS app may find itself in:

- Not running
- Inactive
- Active
- Background
- Suspended

Common State Transitions

The five possible states that a watchOS app finds itself in are represented by the grey boxes in the following image:

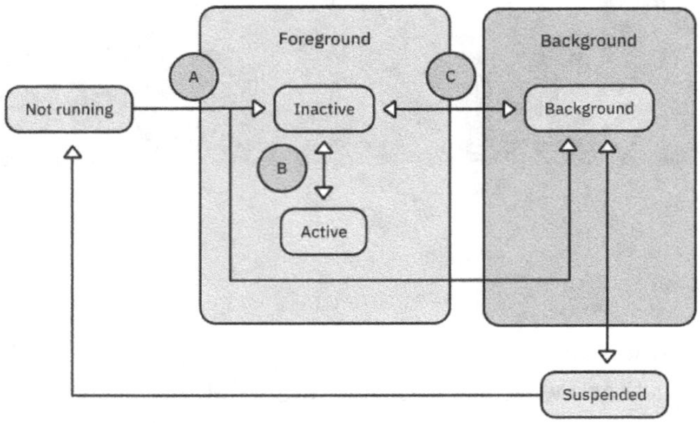

As a developer, you'll only interact with three of the states. The *not running* and *suspended* states are only active, pun intended :], when your app is not running.

Launching to the Active State

If the user has yet to run the app or the system purged the app from memory, the app begins in the *not running* state. Once the app launches, it follows path *A* and transitions to the *inactive* state.

While in the inactive state, the app still runs in the foreground but doesn't receive any actions from the user. However, the app may still be executing code. Don't let the name trick you into thinking the app can't work while in this state.

Almost immediately, the app will follow path *B* and transition to the *active* state, which is the normal mode for apps running on the screen. When in the active state, the app can receive actions from the physical controls on the Apple Watch and user gestures.

When the user starts your app, and it's not already running, watchOS will perform these actions:

- Call `applicationDidFinishLaunching()` and set the `scenePhase` to `.inactive`.
- Create the app's initial scene and the root view.
- Call `applicationWillEnterForeground()`.
- Call `applicationDidBecomeActive()` and set the `scenePhase` to `.active`.
- The app will appear on the screen, and then watchOS will call the root view's `onAppear(perform:)`.

> **Note**: As of watchOS 7 and later, the `scenePhase` environment variable is preferred over the `WKExtensionDelegate` methods when using SwiftUI.

> **Note**: watchOS will not call any `WKExtensionDelegate` lifecycle methods other than `applicationDidFinishLaunching()` for events unrelated to the main interface. Things like complications and notifications will not trigger lifecycle events.

Transitioning to an Inactive State

As soon as the user lowers their arm, they're no longer actively using the app. At that point, watchOS will change to the *inactive* state. As previously mentioned, the app is still running and executing your code. Having your app still running, even though it's in an inactive state, is a point of confusion for many new watchOS developers.

The inactive state is a great time to reduce your app's impact on the Apple Watch's battery. You should pause any battery-intensive actions which don't need to continue. For example, you may be able to disable any active animations that are currently running.

You might also consider whether there's any active state you need to save. Does it make sense to save your **Core Data** stack? Should you write anything to `UserDefaults`?

While your immediate thought is likely *yes*, consider the usage model of your app. As soon as the user lifts their arm again, the app will become active. Therefore, making too many saves might have more of an impact on the battery's life.

When your app transitions to the inactive state, watchOS will set `scenePhase` to `.inactive` and then call `WKExtensionDelegate`'s `applicationWillResignActive()`.

Transitioning to the Background

Two minutes after transitioning to the inactive state, or when the user switches to another app, your app will transition to the *background* state. By following the lower part of path *A*, you can also launch the app directly to the background mode via the system. Background sessions and background tasks will both launch an app directly to the background state.

The OS gives background apps a small but non-deterministic amount of time before the app suspends.

If your app has transitioned to the background state by following path *C*, you'll want to quickly perform whatever necessary actions to recreate the current app state.

You may use the SwiftUI `scenePhase` or `WKExtensionDelegate`'s `applicationDidEnterBackground()` to determine when your app has transitioned to the background.

When transitioning from the inactive state to the background state, watchOS will set `scenePhase` to `.background` and then call `applicationDidEnterBackground()`. Should it require more resources, watchOS will eventually suspend the app.

Returning to Clock

Before watchOS 7, you could ask for eight minutes before your app transitioned to the background. Your app can no longer make that change because developers kept forgetting to set it back to two minutes.

Now the *user* can control the timeout by going to **Settings ▸ General ▸ Return to Clock** on the Apple Watch. There are three options that they can choose:

1. Always.
2. After 2 minutes.
3. After 1 hour.

The default is two minutes. The user may also set the time at an individual app level. As part of your documentation, you may wish to tell the user how to change the setting to one hour for your app if the expectation is that they'll frequently interact with your app outside of the two-minute timeout.

Additional Background Execution Time

If the amount of work you need to perform when transitioning to the background takes more time than watchOS provides your app, you need to rethink what you're doing. For example, this is not the time to make a network call. If you've performed all the optimizations you can and still need a bit more processing time, you can call the `performExpiringActivity(withReason:using:)` method of the `ProcessInfo` class.

If called while your app is in the foreground, you'll get 30 seconds. If called when in the background, you'll receive ten seconds.

The system will asynchronously try to perform the block of code you provide to the `using` parameter. It will then return a boolean value, letting you know whether or not the process is about to suspend.

If you receive a value of `false`, then you may perform your activities as quickly as possible. On the other hand, if you receive a `true` value, the system won't provide you extra time and you need to stop immediately.

Note that just because the system lets you start your extra work, that doesn't mean it will give you enough time to complete it. If your block of code is still running, and the OS needs to suspend your app, then your block of code will be called a second time with the `true` parameter. Your code should be able to handle this cancellation request.

For example, you could check before each action whether watchOS has told you to stop your work. Assuming you had a boolean instance property `cancel`, you might do something like this:

```
processInfo.performExpiringActivity(
  withReason: "I'm really slow"
) { suspending in
  // 1
  guard !suspending else {
    cancel = true
    return
  }

  // 2
```

```
    guard !cancel else { return }
    try? managedObjectContext.save()

    // 3
    guard !cancel else { return }
    userDefaults.set(someData(), forKey: "criticalData")
}
```

In the preceding code, you:

1. Immediately check if you're allowed to run. If the system tells you to suspend, then you set your `cancel` property to true.
2. Before trying to save your Core Data model, ensure that `cancel` is not set. Another thread might have called this same method with a request to suspend.
3. Before saving to `UserDefaults`, check if the OS told you to stop.

It may look a bit odd to check for cancellation each time, but doing so ensures you honor the OS's directions. In the given example, you simply stop when told. In a production app, you may need to do something else *quickly* to flag that you couldn't complete the desired action.

Transitioning Back to the Active State

If the user interacts with the app while it's in the background state, watchOS will transition it back to active via this process:

- Restart the app in the `.background` state.
- Call `applicationWillEnterForeground()`.
- Set the `scenePhase` to `.active`.
- Call `applicationDidBecomeActive()`.

If you've been paying attention, you're likely confused by how the user could interact with the app while it's in the background state. The answer, of course, is that they tap the complication that you provided!

Transitioning to the Suspended State

When your app finally transitions to the *suspended* state, all code execution stops. Your app is still in memory but is not processing events. The system will transition your app to the suspended state when your app is in the background and doesn't have any pending tasks to complete.

Once your app has moved to a suspended state, it's eligible for purging. If the OS needs more memory, it may, without notice, purge any apps that are in a suspended state from memory. Just because your app has moved to a suspended state doesn't mean it *will* be purged, only that it's *eligible* for purging.

The system will do its best not to purge the most recently executed app, any apps in the Dock and any apps that have a complication on the currently active watch face. If the system must purge one of the aforementioned apps, it'll relaunch the app when memory becomes available.

Always On State

Until watchOS 6, the Apple Watch would appear to go to sleep when the user had not recently interacted with it. **Always On** state changed that so that the watch continued to display the time. However, watchOS would blur the currently running app and show the time over your app's display.

Now, by default, your app's user interface displays instead of the time. watchOS won't blur it as long as it's either the frontmost app or running a background session. When in the Always On state, the watch will dim, and the UI will update slower to preserve battery life.

If the user interacts with your app, the system will return to its active state. One noticeable advantage of Always On relates to dates and times. If your app displays a timer, an offset or a relative date, the UI will continue to update with the correct value.

If you wish to disable Always On for your app, simply set the `WKSupportsAlwaysOnDisplay` key to false in the Watch App's **Info.plist**.

> **Note**: Users can disable *Always On* for your app, or the entire device, by going to **Settings ▸ Display & Brightness ▸ Always On**.

State Change Sample

The sample materials for this chapter contain a **Lifecycle** project which you can run against a physical device to observe state changes. When you raise and lower your wrist, you'll see the state changing between active and inactive. If you leave the app inactive for two minutes, you'll notice it switching to background mode.

Extended Runtime Sessions

It's possible to keep your app running, sometimes even while in the background, for four specific types of use cases.

Self Care

Apps focused on the user's emotional well-being or health will run in the foreground, even when the watch screen isn't on. watchOS will give your app a *10 minute* session that will continue until the user switches to another app or you invalidate the session.

Mindfulness

Silent meditation has become a popular practice in recent years. Like self-care, mindfulness apps will stay in the foreground. Meditation is a time-consuming process, though, so watchOS will give your app a *1 hour* session.

If you wish to play audio during the meditation session, you shouldn't use an extended runtime session. Instead, enable background audio and use an `AVAudioSession` as that will keep your app alive. However, it's probably not the best time to play your favorite thrash metal band! :]

Physical Therapy

Stretching, strengthening and range-of-motion exercises are perfect for a **physical therapy** session. Unlike the last two session types, physical therapy sessions run in the *background*. A background session will run until the time limit expires or the app invalidates the session, even if the user launches another app.

Physical therapy sessions can run for up to *1 hour*. PTs are expensive, and Apple knows you can't afford more than an hour-long session.

Smart Alarm

Smart alarms are a great option when you need to schedule a time to check the user's heart rate and motion. You'll get a *30 minute* session for your watch to run in the *background*.

Unlike the other three session types, you must schedule smart alarms to start in the future. You need to start the session within the next 36 hours and schedule it while your app is in the `WKApplicationState.active` state. Your app will likely suspend or terminate, but the session will continue.

When it's time to handle the session, watchOS will call your `WKExtensionDelegate`'s `handle(_:)`.

> **Note**: You must set the session's `delegate` before the handler exits, or your session will terminate.

Once the session is running, you must trigger an alarm by calling the session's `notifyUser(hapticType:repeatHandler:)`. If you forget, watchOS will display a warning and offer to disable future sessions.

Brush Your Teeth

If you have children, you know what a chore it can be to get them to brush their teeth. Not only do you have to convince them to *start* brushing, but then they have to brush for the full two minutes recommended by most dentists. Seems like a great job for an Apple Watch app!

Open **Toothbrush.xcodeproj** from this chapter's starter materials.

Assigning a Session Type

Brushing teeth falls into the self-care session type, but Xcode doesn't know that unless you tell it. Following the steps in the image below, add a new capability to your Watch App target. First, select the **Toothbrush** app from the Project Navigator menu. Next, select the **Toothbrush Watch App** Target. Then, choose **Signing & Capabilities** from the main view and press the **+ Capability** option. Finally, select **Background Modes** from the list of capabilities when prompted.

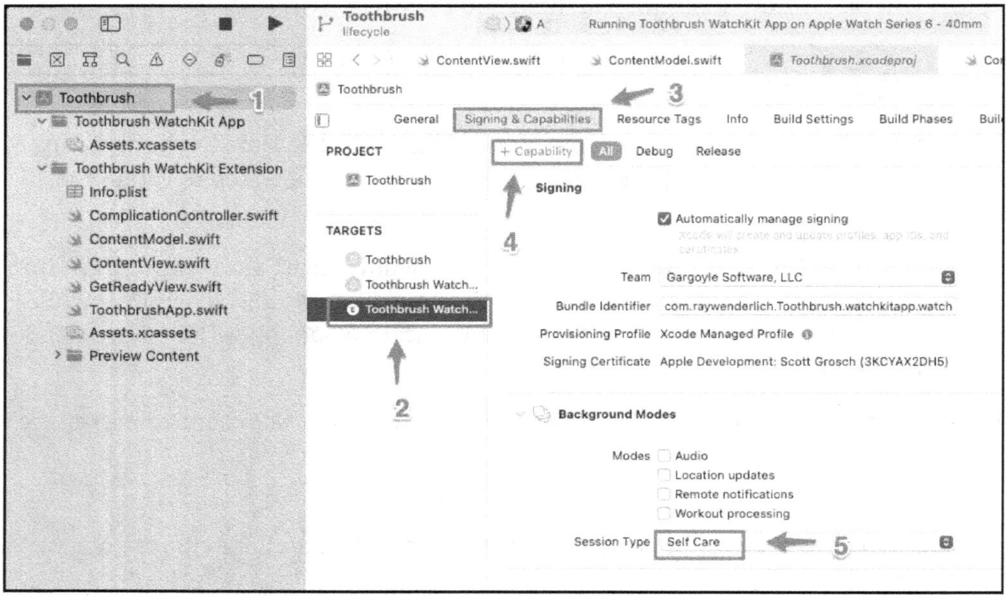

The Content Model

Create a new file named **ContentModel**. Add:

```
import SwiftUI

// 1
final class ContentModel: NSObject, ObservableObject {
  // 2
  @Published var roundsLeft = 0
  @Published var endOfRound: Date?
  @Published var endOfBrushing: Date?

  // 3
  private var timer: Timer!
  private var session: WKExtendedRuntimeSession!
}
```

In the preceding code:

1. You need to conform to `ObservableObject` so the model can update the `ContentView`. You also need to subclass `NSObject` because it's a requirement for conforming to `WKExtendedRuntimeSessionDelegate`, which you'll add in just a bit.
2. The first three properties are `@Published` so `ContentView` responds to updates. You'll use them to track how long you still have to brush.
3. Finally, you need a way to know when time is up, and control the session.

Once the user starts brushing their teeth, you'll need to create the session and update the text displayed on the watch face's button. Add this to `ContentModel`:

```
func startBrushing() {
  session = WKExtendedRuntimeSession()
  session.delegate = self
  session.start()
}
```

You know how picky Xcode is about protocol conformance. So, add the following code to the end of the file to resolve the error that assigning the delegate caused:

```
extension ContentModel: WKExtendedRuntimeSessionDelegate {
  // 1
  func extendedRuntimeSessionDidStart(
    _ extendedRuntimeSession: WKExtendedRuntimeSession
  ) {
  }

  // 2
  func extendedRuntimeSessionWillExpire(
    _ extendedRuntimeSession: WKExtendedRuntimeSession
  ) {
  }

  // 3
  func extendedRuntimeSession(
    _ extendedRuntimeSession: WKExtendedRuntimeSession,
    didInvalidateWith reason:
WKExtendedRuntimeSessionInvalidationReason,
    error: Error?
  ) {
  }
}
```

Conforming to the protocol is pretty simple:

1. The system calls `extendedRuntimeSessionDidStart(_:)` once the session starts running.
2. watchOS will call `extendedRuntimeSessionWillExpire(_:)` just before forcibly expiring your session if your app is about to exceed the session's time limit.
3. Finally, watchOS calls `extendedRuntimeSession(_:didInvalidateWith:error:)` when the session completes for whatever reason.

Notice that the timer wasn't initialized in `startBrushing()`. Until the session is running, you shouldn't start counting down the time. Instead, you'll want to perform startup actions in the delegate method.

Inside `extendedRuntimeSessionDidStart(_:)`, add:

```
let secondsPerRound = 30.0
let now = Date.now

// 1
endOfRound = now.addingTimeInterval(secondsPerRound)
endOfBrushing = now.addingTimeInterval(secondsPerRound * 4)

roundsLeft = 4

// 2
let device = WKInterfaceDevice.current()
device.play(.start)
```

Startup code is mostly straightforward:

1. This is one of the few instances where it's valid to add several seconds instead of performing calendrical operations. You don't care about the actual date or time: you just want a specific number of seconds.
2. When the session starts, it's nice to have the watch perform a quick vibration.

Also, note that both dates are based on the same `now` moment. While unlikely, it's possible that the second of the two date assignments changes, resulting in incorrect calculations.

Now that you know how long each round of brushing will take, it's time to set up a `Timer`. Add the code below to finish out the method:

```
// 1
timer = Timer(
  fire: endOfRound!,
  interval: secondsPerRound,
  repeats: true
) { _ in
  self.roundsLeft -= 1

  // 2
  guard self.roundsLeft == 0 else {
    self.endOfRound =
Date.now.addingTimeInterval(secondsPerRound)
    device.play(.success)
    return
  }

  // 3
  device.play(.success)
  device.play(.success)
}

// 4
RunLoop.main.add(timer, forMode: .common)
```

Here's what the code does:

1. You generate a timer that starts at the end of the current round and repeats every `secondsPerRound` seconds.

2. If there are still rounds of brushing left to perform, you update the time that the round ends so the view's display updates. Having the watch vibrate lets the user know it's time to switch to a new section of their mouth.

3. If the final round is complete, you perform two vibrations to let your kid know they can finally stop their onerous chore.

4. Finally, you schedule the timer into the main run loop.

Did you spot the issue with the preceding code? While you signaled the user via the vibrations that they finished brushing, you didn't let watchOS know you were done. In 30 seconds, they'll get tapped again.

When the last round is complete, you need to perform cleanup:

- Disable the timer.
- Stop the extended runtime session.
- Update the UI.

The `extendedRuntimeSession(_:didInvalidateWith:error:)` seems like the obvious location for cleanup. Right before step three in the code above, cancel the session:

```
extendedRuntimeSession.invalidate()
```

When you invalidate the session, watchOS will call that delegate method. Add the following code to `extendedRuntimeSession(_:didInvalidateWith:error:)`:

```
timer.invalidate()
timer = nil

endOfRound = nil
endOfBrushing = nil
roundsLeft = 0
```

Build your project to make sure you've entered everything properly so far. Now it's time to handle the UI.

The Content View

Edit **ContentView**, and you'll see that it's already configured to print the `ScenePhase` for you during phase updates. The first task required is, of course, to use the model you just created. So, add the following line to the view:

```
@ObservedObject private var model = ContentModel()
```

Using an `@ObservedObject`, SwiftUI will update the `body` any time one of the published variables from your model updates. Next, replace the default `Text("Hello, World!")` in the `body` (don't remove `.onChange(of:)`) with:

```
// 1
VStack {
  // 2
  Button {
    model.startBrushing()
  } label: {
    Text("Start brushing")
  }
```

```
    .disabled(model.roundsLeft != 0)
    .padding()

    // 3
    if let endOfBrushing = model.endOfBrushing,
       let endOfRound = model.endOfRound {
      Text("Rounds Left: \(model.roundsLeft - 1)")
      Text("Total time left: \(endOfBrushing, style: .timer)")
      Text("This round time left: \(endOfRound, style: .timer)")
    }
  }
```

In the preceding code:

1. Using a `VStack` lets you place multiple views in a vertical layout.
2. When the user taps **Start brushing**, you'll begin the process by calling into your model. Be sure to disable the button if they're already brushing!
3. If there are dates set in the model, that means a session is active, and you'll therefore want to let the user know how much time is left. Take note of the `style: .timer` modifier in the string interpolation, which may be new syntax to you. Instead of displaying a date, SwiftUI will automatically update a countdown timer.

Build and run the app on a *physical device*. While you could run in the simulator, the scene phase will never switch to inactive or background if you do.

Once you tap the button, you'll see the countdown begin:

Activate the console by pressing **Shift-Command-C**. Then clear out all unhelpful debugging information Xcode emits by default by pressing **Control-K**.

Lift and lower your arm a few times, and you'll see messages in the console that the app has switched to the active or inactive states. However, the app never moves to the background, even though you'll eventually pass the two-minute mark. The session has kept the app alive.

Ready, Set, Go

While functional, you can do better! Have you ever used the **Workout** app on your watch? When you start a workout, you get a few seconds to get ready before it begins. That seems useful for your app as well. The starter sample contains **GetReadyView** that simulates that display.

In **ContentModel**, add another property:

```
@Published var showGettingReady = false
```

By default, the getting ready timer shouldn't display. You'll also want to set it to false once brushing has started. So, add this as the first line of `startBrushing()`:

```
showGettingReady = false
```

Then, back in **ContentView**, replace the call to `model.startBrushing()` with:

```
model.showGettingReady = true
```

To make something happen when you tell the timer to display, add an overlay modifier to the `VStask` immediately before the `.onChange(of:)` call:

```
// 1
.overlay(
  // 2
  VStack {
    if model.showGettingReady {
      // 3
      GetReadyView {
        model.startBrushing()
      }
      .frame(width: 125, height: 125)
      .padding()
    } else {
      // 4
      EmptyView()
    }
  }
)
```

Cool stuff happening:

1. An `overlay` layers a secondary view in front of another view.
2. By using a `VStack`, even though you're only going to show a single view, you gain the ability to display a timer conditionally.
3. If you asked to show it, then you provide the `GetReadyView`. The closure is called when the countdown is complete, at which point it's time to start brushing.
4. By using the `EmptyView`, you don't display anything, but SwiftUI is still happy about the conditional check.

Build and rerun the app. This time, you'll get a couple of seconds to get ready:

Key Points

- An inactive phase on watchOS doesn't mean the app isn't running.
- Prefer SwiftUI's `.scenePhase` environment variable over extension delegate methods.
- For specific types of apps, extended runtimes let your app keep running even when in the background.

Where to Go From Here?

Check out Apple's documentation for WatchKit Life Cycles (https://apple.co/2WTQgyR) and Extended Runtime Sessions (https://apple.co/2WPvCA3).

Chapter 8: Complications

By Scott Grosch

Exploring the Sample

Please build and run the **TideWatch** app from this chapter's starter materials. After a moment, you'll see current tide conditions at the Point Reyes tide station in California.

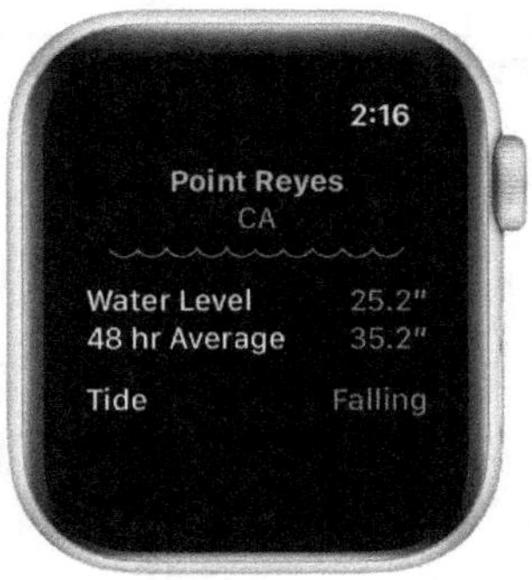

Tap the station name to pick a new location:

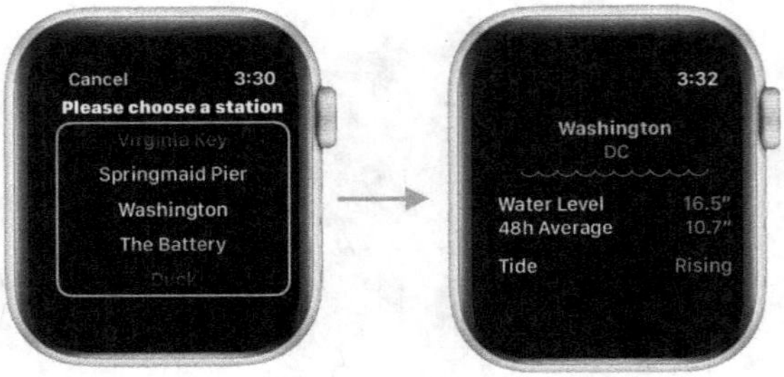

Though the app is useful as designed, your customers have to open the app to find the current water level. Wouldn't it be better if they could see the information right on their watch face?

Adding a Widget Extension

In Xcode, choose **File ▸ New ▸ Target...**, then select **Widget Extension** from the **watchOS** tab. For the **Product Name**, enter **TideWatch Widget**. Be sure to select **Include Configuration Intent** if it's not already selected:

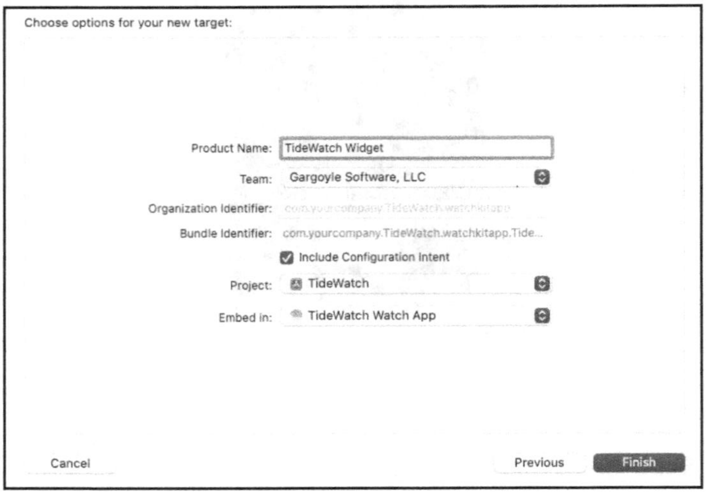

Xcode will place all of the widget-related code into a single file named **TideWatch_Widget**. The first thing you'll want to do is separate the single file into individual files. The rest of this chapter will assume you've done so and refer to the files accordingly.

> **Note**: The current version of Xcode gets confused and will make the target membership of your new files **TideWatch Watch App** instead of **TideWatch WidgetExtension**, resulting in numerous compiler errors.

You'll end up with a structure that looks like this:

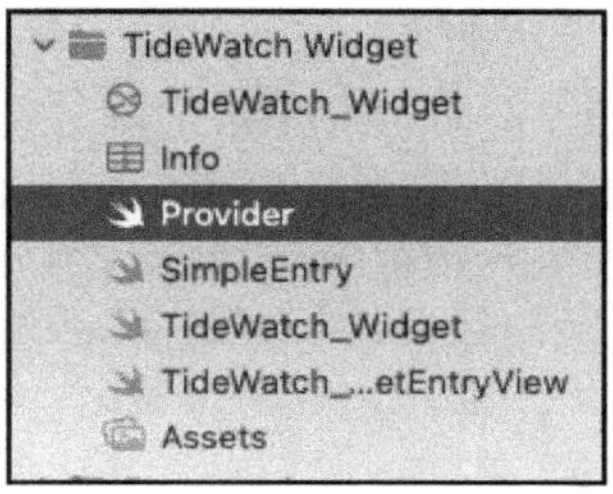

In **Provider**, edit the signature of `getTimeline(for:in:completion:)`. The generic parameter `Entry` needs to be updated to say `SimpleEntry` to resolve the compiler error.****

Ensure your project builds without problems before moving on.

If, by chance, you decide to name your project **Widget**, you'll get a confusing compiler error due to the existing protocol of the same name. If you wish to use "Widget" as the name of your project, you'll need to explicitly include the full protocol name:

```
struct Widget: SwiftUI.Widget {
```

Timeline Provider

When watchOS wants to update the data displayed for your widget, it'll look to your timeline provider. watchOS expects you to provide either an `IntentTimelineProvider` or `TimelineProvider` struct. The former should be used when you wish to allow configuration of your widgets, such as picking what tide station is displayed. The latter will be used when there are no options to choose.

Both protocols expect you to implement four methods.

placeholder(in:)

When the user selects your widget, watchOS needs some type of placeholder data to present. Use `placeholder(in:)` to provide whatever is appropriate for your widget. Note that you should not perform any expensive operations in this method. Just generate some random data as quickly as possible.

getSnapshot(for:in:completion:)

When watchOS is transitioning between views, this method will be called. You can use this method to present real data based on the selection if you wish. If you can determine the "current" data promptly, then show real data. Otherwise, just return placeholder data. Remember, the person will only be on the edit screen for a few moments, so not having *correct* data isn't a concern.

getTimeline(for:in:completion:)

Widgets will update the data presented at specific moments. You use the `getTimeline(for:in:completion:)` method to let watchOS know precisely what data should be used at what time.

recommendations

When using widgets with iOS, a configuration is done through the **intentdefinition** file. Unfortunately, watchOS does not support the same level of configuration. Instead, use the`recommendations` method to return each specific configuration that you support.

Shared Code

The starter project includes a **Shared** folder containing code used by both the primary app and the extension. Please select all files within the **Shared** folder and add the widget extension to their target membership.

Configure the Widget

Switch the active scheme to **TideWatch WidgetExtension** and then **build and run** again. Using the widget scheme will launch the simulator directly to the watch face.

Tap and hold on the watch face, and the editor will appear:

Tap **Edit**, then swipe left three times so you can pick the complication you want to replace:

Tap one of the corner locations to see the list of complications you may choose from:

Finally, scroll to the bottom to see your complication:

That doesn't look great. Let's make it useful!

Configuring the Display

Look in **TideWatch_Widget** and you'll see the defaults that Xcode used when populating the `body`. The `configurationDisplayName` and `description` modifiers are part of WatchKit, but appear to not have any effect with watchOS. However, that'll likely change in a future version, so put better values there:

```
.configurationDisplayName("TideWatch")
.description("Show current tide conditions.")
```

This `Widget` is just a wrapper around `TideWatch_WidgetEntryView`. I feel that the name is too long, so open **TideWatch_WidgetEntryView**. That's a long name, so I'll rename it to just **EntryView**. Right-click on `TideWatch_WidgetEntryView`, then choose **Refactor ▸ Rename...**. For the new name, use `EntryView`. Switch to the **EntryView** file.

A complication can show four types of displays, known as a **family**. You'll need to present different information depending on which family the user selects.

Accessory Corner

The Metropolitan watch face contains four corner locations that you can select, known as the accessory corner family. Create a new SwiftUI View file named **AccessoryCornerView** and paste the following contents:

```
import SwiftUI
import WidgetKit

struct AccessoryCornerView: View {
  // 1
  let tide: Tide

  var body: some View {
    // 2
    tide.image()
      // 3
      .widgetLabel {
        Text(tide.heightString(unitStyle: .long))
      }
  }
}

struct AccessoryCornerView_Previews: PreviewProvider {
  static var previews: some View {
    // 4
    AccessoryCornerView(tide: Tide.placeholder())
      // 5
```

```
        .previewContext(WidgetPreviewContext(family: .accessoryCor
ner))
    }
}
```

In the preceding code:

1. Your complication will always take some data model. For the sample project, that's a `Tide`.
2. The type of tide is represented with an image. That image is what will appear in the corner of the complication's display.
3. When using an accessory corner, you'll want the text to curve with the display. You accomplish that by placing your text inside a `widgetLabel` modifier.
4. The provided `Tide` model includes a convenient `placeholder` function to generate fake data.
5. You specify that the preview is for a `WidgetPreviewContext` and explicitly state which family is being used.

Looking at the canvas in the top left, you'll see what your complication will look like:

The image is tiny and is just floating in space. Replace the image line with this:

```
ZStack {
  AccessoryWidgetBackground()
  tide.image()
    .font(.title.bold())
}
```

Now you end up with something nicer:

By setting a `.title.bold()` font, you've increased the visibility of the image, and placing an `AccessoryWidgetBackground` below it adds a nice circular backdrop.

You'll create a few of these views, so in **TideWatch Widget**, create a group called **Templates** to put them in. Move **AccessoryCornerView** into that group and add the rest as you create them.

Accessory Circular

Create another SwiftUI View named **AccessoryCircularView**, using the following contents:

```
import SwiftUI
import WidgetKit

struct AccessoryCircularView: View {
  var tide: Tide

  var body: some View {
    VStack {
      tide.image()
        .font(.title.bold())

      Text(tide.heightString())
        .font(.headline)
        .foregroundColor(.blue)
    }
  }
}

struct AccessoryCircularView_Previews: PreviewProvider {
  static var previews: some View {
    AccessoryCircularView(tide: Tide.placeholder())
      .previewContext(WidgetPreviewContext(family: .accessoryCir
cular))
  }
}
```

The circular view presents a small area to display your data. For the TideWatch app, it makes sense to put an image above the text. Using a `headline` font makes for a nice size and spruces things up with a blue color. I hope your water is blue.

Notice that you're specifying the `accessoryCircular` value in the preview provider.

The accessory circular view is used in many watch faces. Some will allow a `widgetLabel` modifier, like what you used in the accessory corner modifier. Others won't. By using the `.showsWidgetLabel` environment property, you can write conditional code to handle both cases.

Two families down, two to go.

Accessory Inline

New to watchOS 9 is the accessory inline family. Many of the watch faces provide an area for a single line of text. Depending on the watch face, the amount of area available differs. In a newly created **AccessoryInlineView** file, paste the following:

```
import SwiftUI
import WidgetKit

struct AccessoryInlineView: View {
  let tide: Tide

  var body: some View {
    Text("\(tide.heightString()) and \(tide.type.rawValue) as of
\(tide.date.formatted(date: .omitted, time: .shortened))")
  }
}

struct AccessoryInline_Previews: PreviewProvider {
  static var previews: some View {
    AccessoryInlineView(tide: Tide.placeholder())
      .previewContext(WidgetPreviewContext(family: .accessoryInl
ine))
  }
}
```

Xcode's preview will display something like this:

Looks great. But on a different type of watch face, you won't have that much space. SwiftUI provides a solution for that, available in watchOS 9. By wrapping text with the new `ViewThatFits` keyword, Xcode will select the text that fully fits in the available space. Replace the contents of `body` with the following:

```
ViewThatFits {
  Text("\(tide.heightString()) and \(tide.type.rawValue) as of \
(tide.date.formatted(date: .omitted, time: .shortened))")
  Text("\(tide.heightString()), \(tide.type.rawValue), \
(tide.date.formatted(date: .omitted, time: .shortened))")
  Text("\(tide.heightString()), \(tide.type.rawValue)")
  Text(tide.heightString())
}
```

Now, depending on the available space, you'll provide appropriate information without the text being chopped.

Accessory Rectangular

The fourth and final complication family is accessory rectangular. The rectangular family provides a large rectangular space available for anything you might need to display, such as a chart, multiple lines of text, etc...

Paste the following into a newly created **AccessoryRectangularView** file:

```
import SwiftUI
import WidgetKit

struct AccessoryRectangularView: View {
  let tide: Tide

  var body: some View {
    HStack {
      VStack(alignment: .leading) {
        Text(tide.heightString(unitStyle: .long))
          .font(.headline)
          .foregroundColor(.blue)
        Text(tide.date.formatted(date: .omitted,
time: .shortened))
          .font(.caption)
        Text(tide.type.rawValue.capitalized)
          .font(.caption)
      }
```

```
        tide.image()
          .font(.headline.bold())
      }
    }
  }

  struct AccessoryRectangularView_Previews: PreviewProvider {
    static var previews: some View {
      AccessoryRectangularView(tide: Tide.placeholder())
        .previewContext(WidgetPreviewContext(family: .accessoryRec
  tangular))
    }
  }
```

The rectangular view accommodates about three lines of text. With this family, you can present the tide height, when the measurement was taken, the type of tide and then include the image representing the tide type:

Now that you've defined views for all of the complication families, you need to tell watchOS how to select the proper one.

Using the Defined Complications

Switch back to **EntryView**. Remember: This is the view the widget will display. watchOS will provide the current family being used through the `widgetFamily` environment value. Add the following property:

```
@Environment(\.widgetFamily) private var family
```

Then, replace the contents of the `body` with a `switch` statement:

```
var body: some View {
  switch family {
  case .accessoryCircular:
    AccessoryCircularView(tide: entry.tide)

  case .accessoryCorner:
    AccessoryCornerView(tide: entry.tide)

  case .accessoryInline:
    AccessoryInlineView(tide: entry.tide)
```

```
    case .accessoryRectangular:
      AccessoryRectangularView(tide: entry.tide)

    @unknown default:
      Text("Unsupported widget")
    }
  }
```

Now, when watchOS needs to display your complication, it'll select the proper view based on the family.

Why the `@unknown default` element? While you've implemented all of the options in your `switch` statement, watchOS 10 might add another family. By having the unknown default you ensure your code doesn't crash.

At this point, you'll see multiple complication errors due to `tide` not being defined. Edit **SimpleEntry** and add a new property:

```
let tide: Tide
```

Next, edit **TideWatch_Widget** and update the preview provider to include the new parameter:

```
EntryView(entry: SimpleEntry(date: Date(), configuration:
ConfigurationIntent(), tide: Tide.placeholder()))
```

Finally, in **Provider**, update all the calls to the `SimpleEntry` constructor to include the tide:

```
SimpleEntry(date: entryDate, configuration: configuration, tide:
Tide.placeholder())
```

The Fruits of Your Labor

Open **TideWatch_Widget** and you'll see one watch face. At the bottom of the window, you'll see an icon with six small squares. Click on that and then choose **Widget Family Variants**. Xcode will update the canvas to include four watch faces, one for each type of widget.

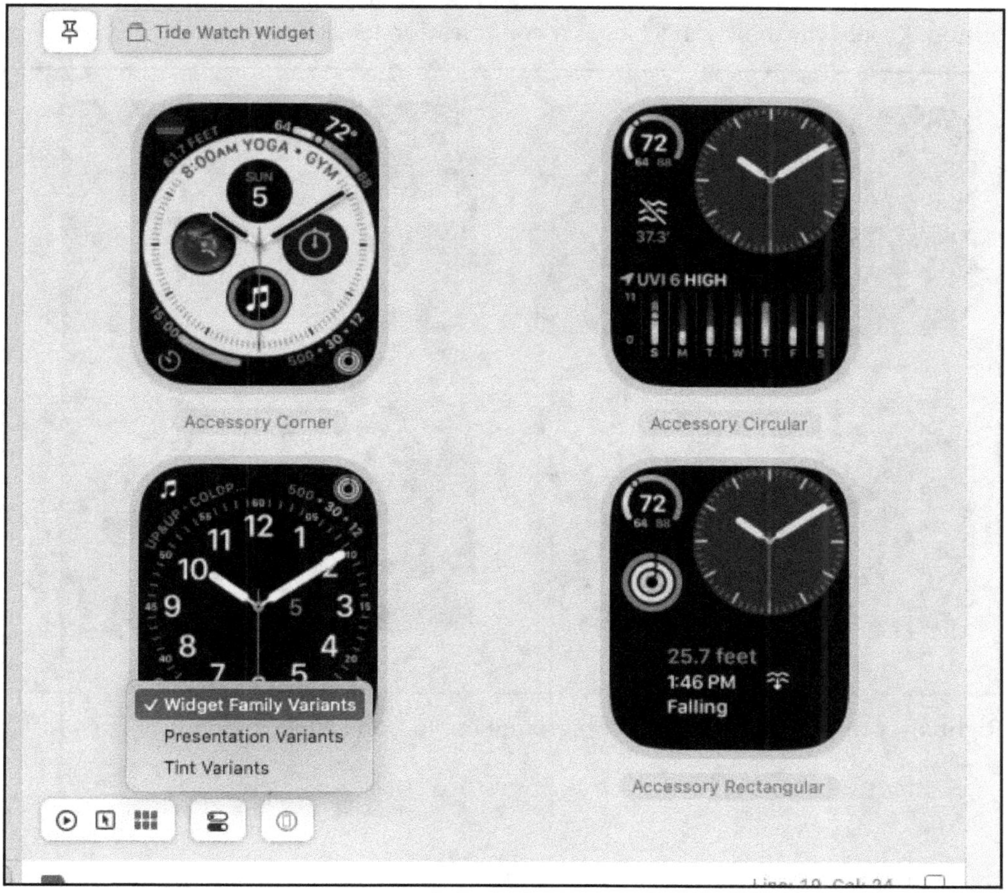

Tinting

You'll notice that instead of picking Widget Family Variants you could have chosen **Tint Variants**. Remember that by default, the Apple Watch is set to full color mode. However, many of your users will instead switch to a tinted theme.

Switch back to the **AccessoryRectangularView** file and then select the Tint Variants option. Xcode will show you what your complication looks like for each color:

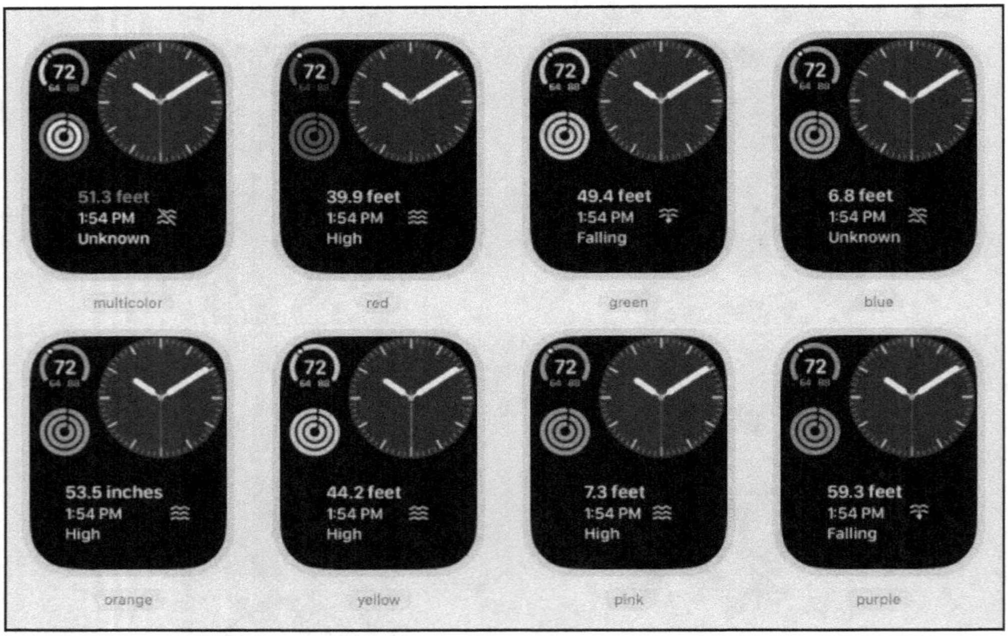

Right after the line that sets the foreground to blue, add a new modifier:

```
.widgetAccentable()
```

Xcode will now show the tide height in the user's selected tint:

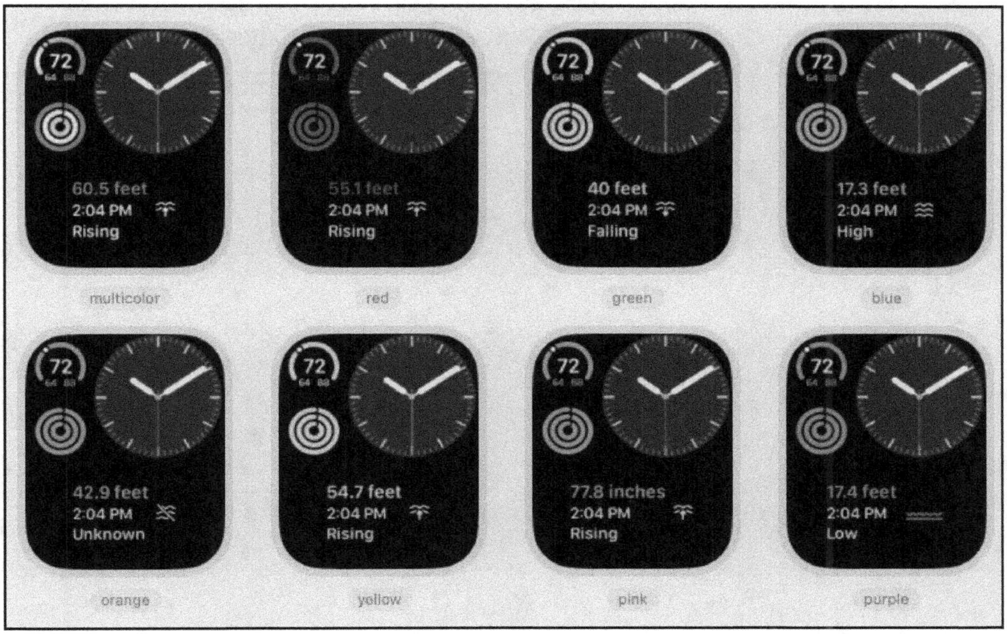

You can apply the modifier to as many items as you wish. You might want, for example, to also apply the tinting to the image.

Station Selection

Now, your users have no way to select which measurement station they'd like to use for the complication. Supporting that isn't hard — it just requires multiple steps.

Configure the Intent

Open the **TideWatch_Widget** file that's not a Swift file. It's the one that looks somewhat like an infinity symbol inside of a circle. If you're familiar with Siri and/or Intents, it'll look familiar. If not, don't fear.

At the bottom of the white part of the Xcode window, click the + button and choose **New Type**, naming the type **StationChoice**.

Next, click on the **Configuration** line and add a parameter named **station**. Set the type to **Station Choice**. Finally, uncheck the **Siri can ask for value when run** checkbox and check the **Options are provided dynamically** checkbox.

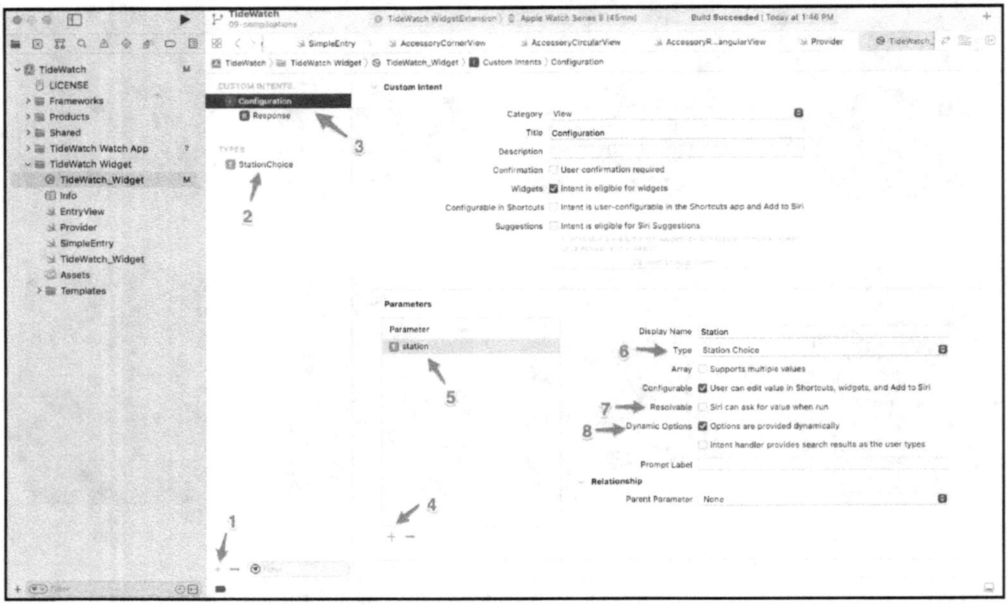

By performing the above steps, you have access to a `station` property on the intent configuration passed to your `Widget`.

Configure the Provider

Now edit the `recommendations()` method, in **Provider**, that was mentioned at the start of the chapter. You must return an intent recommendation for every element you wish the user to be able to select when adding your complication. In this case, that means one item per measurement station.

Replace the body of the `recommendations` method with the following code:

```
// 1
return MeasurementStation
  .allStations
  // 2
  .map { station in
    // 3
    let intent = ConfigurationIntent()

    // 4
    intent.station = StationChoice(identifier: station.id,
```

```
display: station.name)

    // 5
    return IntentRecommendation(intent: intent, description:
station.name)
  }
```

Here's what's happening:

1. You're returning data from the `MeasurementStation` class that knows about the various locations you can display data against.
2. Each of the `MeasurementStation` objects needs to be transformed to a new type, so you're passing the array through a `map`.
3. The method signature says you'll be returning objects of type `ConfigurationIntent`, so create one :]
4. Xcode created a `StationChoice` intent object for you based on adding the `StationChoice` type in the intent configuration.
5. Finally, you return the new recommendation, providing the intent. The **description** parameter is what will be used for the name when selecting the complication.

If you build and run, look at the available complications again. You'll see new choices:

watchOS will only display a few choices for your app, then will add a **More** button that allows you to pick the rest of the stations. Pick one of the stations and go back to the watch face to see the data for that station.

Starting Properly

You have one last piece to handle. When you tap on a complication, your app is launched. Ensure that the proper measurement station is selected at startup.

Edit **EntryView** and add the following method:

```
private func url() -> URL {
  guard let stationId = entry.configuration.station?.identifier
else {
    return URL(string: "tidewatch://station/NOTASTATION")!
  }

  return URL(string: "tidewatch://station/\(stationId)")!
}
```

By looking at the `entry.configuration` property, you have access to the selected station. By using the given `identifier` you create a deep link URL for your app.

Next, tell the views to use that URL by adding the following modifier to *each* of the accessory views in `EntryView`:

```
.widgetURL(url())
```

For example:

```
AccessoryCircularView(tide: entry.tide)
  .widgetURL(url())
```

Build and run again. When you tap the complication, the `widgetURL` call sets the URL to open in the containing app, which is your watchOS app.

Finally, edit **ContentView** in the **TideWatch Watch App**. At the end of the body, add one more modifier:

```
// 1
.onOpenURL { url in
  // 2
  let stationId = url.lastPathComponent

  // 3
  guard
    url.scheme == "tidewatch",
    url.host == "station",
    stationId != "/",
    !stationId.isEmpty
  else {
    return
  }

  // 4
  if let station = MeasurementStation.station(for: stationId) {
    Task { await model.fetch(newStation: station) }
  }
}
```

It's relatively straightforward:

1. `onOpenURL` triggers when the view receives a URL.
2. The URL you're sending expects the last element to be the station ID.
3. Validate that the URL scheme and the host are correct, and that you've actually received a station identifier.
4. If the provided station identifier is known, then call code to fetch the data for that station and update the display.

In this sample project, some lag occurs as the station data is downloaded again at open. In a production app, you'd likely have the current data cached somewhere, or maybe you pass it in as part of the URL configuration.

Privacy and Luminance

When the watch goes inactive on watches that have an always-on display, it switches to a low luminance mode. By default, the content isn't redacted in a low luminance state. However, users can modify that setting.

Use the `.isLuminanceReduced` environment variable to determine whether the Apple Watch has moved into an always-on state with the luminance reduced. Depending on what is displayed via your complication, you might wish to change what is visible in this state.

Remove any time-sensitive content, such as counters, when in low luminance. Updates will not happen as frequently, meaning your values will be wrong.

You'll also want to redact sensitive information at times. By default, privacy mode will show a redacted version of your placeholder view. It's possible, however, that not everything is sensitive content. If that's the case, you might apply the `.privacySensitive()` modifier to those elements that should not be shown. Other content on the complication will then still be visible when in redacted mode.

Freshness

Great work! You implemented your first complication. Have you noticed the issue with the data? You never provided content.

In the next chapter, you'll learn how to provide data and keep it up-to-date.

Chapter 9: Keeping Complications Updated

By Scott Grosch

Now that your complications are available to place on the watch face, you have one last consideration. How do you ensure the displayed data is up to date?

Background Download

When your complication's timeline runs out of data, or even before, you'll want to initiate a background download. While your first instinct is likely to call one of the `dataTask` methods from `URLSession`, that won't work. watchOS might pause and restart your widget extension multiple times during the download. Instead, you'll have to create a download task.

Refactor CoOpsApi

Now that both the app and the widget extension need to download data, you'll need to move some files from **TideWatch Watch App** into **Shared**. The main file you need is **CoOpsApi**, but moving it has a cascading effect. Move the **CurrentTideKeys** file, as well as the **Download** and **Extensions** folders into **Shared**.

> **Note**: Add the newly moved files to the widget extension's target membership.

Build your project to ensure the moved files all have the correct target membership.

A few refactorings are required to support downloading data from both projects. The first step you should perform is to declare a property for the root URL in **CoOpsApi**:

```
private let rootUrl = "https://api.tidesandcurrents.noaa.gov/
api/prod/datagetter"
```

Mode the assignment of `components.queryItems` from `url(for:)` into a method of its own:

```
private func queryItems(
  for stationId: MeasurementStation.ID,
  from start: Date, to end: Date
) -> [URLQueryItem] {
  return [
    "product": "predictions",
    "units": "metric",
    "time_zone": "gmt",
    "application": "TideWatch",
    "format": "json",
    "datum": "mllw",
    "interval": "h",
    "station": stationId,
    "begin_date": "\
(Formatters.predictionInputFormatter.string(from: start))",
    "end_date": "\
(Formatters.predictionInputFormatter.string(from: end))"
  ].map { .init(name: $0.key, value: $0.value) }
}
```

Then call that method instead in `url(for:)`:

```
components.queryItems = queryItems(for: stationId, from: start,
to: end)
```

While still in `url(for:)`, use the new property in the `guard` clause:

```
var components = URLComponents(string: rootUrl)
```

The widget extension needs a method to call to initiate a download, so create that next:

```
public func getWidgetData(
  for stationId: MeasurementStation.ID,
  using session: URLSession
) {
  let end = Calendar.utc.date(byAdding: .hour, value: 1, to:
Date.now)!

  var components = URLComponents(string: rootUrl)!
  components.queryItems = queryItems(for: stationId, from:
Date.now, to: end)

  let request = URLRequest(url: components.url!)
  session
    .downloadTask(with: request)
    .resume()
}
```

While the main app can perform a normal data download, as previously mentioned, the widget extension needs to use a `downloadTask`.

The final change required in the **CoOpsApi** file is to make the decoding method public, since it now gets called from the widget extension as well. Add one last method to decode the download data:

```
public func decodeTide(_ data: Data?) -> [Tide] {
  let decoder = JSONDecoder()
  decoder.dateDecodingStrategy
= .formatted(Formatters.predictionOutputFormatter)

  guard
    let data,
    let results = try? decoder.decode(TidePredictions.self,
from: data),
    let predictions = results.predictions
  else {
    return []
  }

  return predictions.map { predication in
    Tide(on: predication.date, at: predication.height)
  }
}
```

Then, in `getLowWaterHeights(for:)`, replace the text from the `JSONDecoder` initializer through the `levels` assignment with a call to the method you just created:

```
let levels = decodeTide(data)
```

That was quite a bit of refactoring, so ensure your project still builds without errors.

Caching Sessions

Apple's developer documentation specifies, in a complicated manner, that you must reuse sessions when possible. Also, you need to reattach any previously interrupted sessions that have started again.

In the **TideWatch Widget** project, create a file named **SessionData** that contains the stored session:

```
import Foundation

final class SessionData {
  let session: URLSession

  init(session: URLSession) {
    self.session = session
  }
}
```

Next, create another file name **SessionCache** to handle the various caching logic:

```
import Foundation

// 1
final class SessionCache: NSObject {
  // 2
  static let shared = SessionCache()

  // 3
  var sessions: [String: SessionData] = [:]

  // 4
  private override init() {}
}
```

In the preceding code:

1. The class will eventually implement session delegates, so ensure it inherits from `NSObject`.
2. Creating a static shared property allows you to use `SessionCache` as a singleton.
3. Because you might have multiple sessions running at once, you need to be able to find the appropriate `URLSession` based on a session identifier.
4. By overriding the `init` method and making it `private`, you ensure that the class can only be used as a singleton, via the `shared` property.

Each time the extension needs to download data, it must either reattach an existing `URLSession` or create one. Add the following helper method:

```
// 1
func sessionData(for stationId: MeasurementStation.ID) ->
SessionData {
  // 2
  if let data = sessions[stationId] {
    return data
  }

  // 3
  let session = URLSession(
    configuration: .background(withIdentifier: stationId),
    delegate: self,
    delegateQueue: nil
  )

  // 4
  let data = SessionData(session: session)
  sessions[stationId] = data

  return data
}
```

Here's what's happening:

1. Given a station identifier, you'll provide the required `SessionData`, which includes the `URLSession`.
2. If cached data for the specified station already exists, simply return that.
3. If there's not, you'll initiate a new background enabled `URLSession`. By specifying the `stationId` as the identifier, you ensure that watchOS can reattach an existing download that was previously terminated.
4. Finally, create a new `SessionData`, store it in the cache and return the object.

Xcode now shows an error as you specified the `SessionCache` as the `delegate`, so add the following to the end of the file to conform to the delegate:

```
extension SessionCache: URLSessionDownloadDelegate {
  func urlSession(
    _ session: URLSession,
    downloadTask: URLSessionDownloadTask,
    didFinishDownloadingTo location: URL
  ) {
  }

  func urlSession(
    _ session: URLSession,
    task: URLSessionTask,
    didCompleteWithError error: Error?
  ) {
  }
}
```

Timeline Provider

It's time to initiate a download. Head back to **Provider** and replace the entire contents of `getTimeLine(for:in:completion:)` with the following code:

```
// 1
let stationId = configuration.station!.identifier!

// 2
let sessionData = SessionCache.shared.sessionData(for:
stationId)

// 3
CoOpsApi.shared.getWidgetData(for: stationId, using:
sessionData.session)
```

Here's why you need that code:

1. When asked for a timeline, watchOS will provide the configuration data that you created in the previous chapter. Specifically, you'll be given `station` that was configured in the **TideWatch_Widget** intent configuration. It's safe to force unwrap because this method won't be called without a station.
2. You pull the appropriate session to use, possibly having created a new session, via the code you just implemented.
3. Finally, watchOS will initiate a background download, using the appropriate session.

While the above is relatively straightforward, a gaping hole is in the code, as provided. Do you see the problem?

Getting a timeline requires calling a completion handler so watchOS knows when the data has been updated. Unfortunately, these methods are not yet `async` aware, so it's time to make some changes to your session code.

Open **SessionData** and add a new property that conforms to the completion handler:

```
var downloadCompletion: (([Tide]) -> Void)? = nil
```

It's a pretty ugly signature, but you've declared an optional property that expects to be provided with an array of `Tide` objects and has no return type.

Back in **Provider**, just before you call the `getWidgetData(for:using:)` method, assign that property:

```
// 1
sessionData.downloadCompletion = { tides in
  // 2
  var entries = tides.map { tide in
    SimpleEntry(date: tide.date, configuration: configuration,
tide: tide)
  }

  // 3
  if entries.isEmpty {
    entries = [SimpleEntry(date: Date.now, configuration:
configuration, tide: nil)]
  }

  // 4
  let oneHour = Calendar.current.date(byAdding: .hour, value: 1,
to: Date.now)!
```

```
    completion(.init(entries: entries, policy: .after(oneHour)))
  }
```

In the preceding code:

1. Every time watchOS requests a new timeline, the delegate that will be called at completion should be updated.
2. The decoded `Tide` data is converted to an array of `SimpleEntry` objects, which watchOS expects to be passed to the completion handler for presentation at the appropriate time.
3. It's important to handle the possibility that no data is available. For instance, the network or the remote server might be down.
4. Finally, you call the completion handler with the new data, specifying that watchOS should ask for the next update one hour from now.

In the previous chapter, you assumed a `Tide` object was always available, but now there isn't, so Xcode is showing compiler errors.

Edit **SimpleEntry** to make the `tide` property optional. Doing so means all of your templates must be updated to handle the case of no data. In this chapter's project materials, I've provided updated versions of the templates that you can copy into your project.

You'll have one last error to fix in **EntryView**. The new template expects you to pass the station name when using an `AccessoryRectangularView`:

```
AccessoryRectangularView(
  tide: entry.tide,
  stationName: entry.configuration.station?.displayString
)
```

Your project should now compile cleanly.

While you've implemented the code for `downloadCompletion`, which calls the required completion handler, nothing yet calls `downloadCompletion`.

Completing the Session

In **SessionCache**, when the delegate methods are complete, you'll need to call the `downloadCompletion` delegate, if it's set. Note that even if the session completed with an error, you *still* need to call the delegate to tell watchOS to complete the timeline. Add a new method, as shown below:

```
private func downloadCompleted(for session: URLSession, data:
Data? = nil) {
  // 1
  guard let stationId = session.configuration.identifier else {
    return
  }

  // 2
  let tides = data == nil ? [] :
CoOpsApi.shared.decodeTide(data)

  // 3
  let sessionData = SessionCache.shared.sessionData(for:
stationId)

  // 4
  DispatchQueue.main.async {
    sessionData.downloadCompletion?(tides)
    sessionData.downloadCompletion = nil
  }
}
```

As you can see, the code is straightforward:

1. Retrieve the `stationId` that was assigned during the `URLSession` creation.
2. Decode the supplied `Data`, if it exists. If it's `nil`, then an error occurred and you simply default to an empty array.
3. Find the `SessionData` so you have access to the delegates.
4. Call the stored `downloadCompletion` on the main thread, if it exists, passing in the decoded tides. While not strictly required, clear out the delegate so it can't be called a second time.

Finally, update the `URLSessionDownloadDelegate` methods:

```
func urlSession(
  _ session: URLSession,
  downloadTask: URLSessionDownloadTask,
  didFinishDownloadingTo location: URL
) {
  // 1
  guard
    location.isFileURL,
    let data = try? Data(contentsOf: location)
  else {
    downloadCompleted(for: session)
    return
  }

  // 2
  downloadCompleted(for: session, data: data)
}

func urlSession(
  _ session: URLSession,
  task: URLSessionTask,
  didCompleteWithError error: Error?
) {
  // 3
  downloadCompleted(for: session)
}
```

In the preceding code:

1. When a download task finishes you'll be provided with a file `URL` pointing to the full contents of the downloaded data. If the provided location isn't a file or watchOS can't read the contents, then you call the `downloadCompleted(for:)` method with data, signifying an error occurred.
2. Otherwise, you pass the data to the completion method for processing.
3. In the case of a download error, call the completion method with no data.

You didn't think you were done, did you?

Background URLSession Events

Background network requests are delivered directly to the widget extension, not the containing app. When a background URL session event occurs, you must tell watchOS whether you're able to process the event, and if so, what to do.

Add a new method to **SessionCache** to determine what identifier is valid:

```
func isValid(for stationId: MeasurementStation.ID) -> Bool {
  return sessions[stationId] != nil
}
```

Next, in **TideWatch_Widget**, add a new modifier to the end of the `body`:

```
.onBackgroundURLSessionEvents { identifier in
  // 1
  return SessionCache.shared.isValid(for: identifier)
} _: { identifier, completion in
  // 2
  let data = SessionCache.shared.sessionData(for: identifier)

  // 3
  data.sessionCompletion = completion
}
```

Upon receiving a session event:

1. Ensure the session's identifier is valid. If it's not, processing will stop.
2. If the identifier was valid, retrieve the `SessionCache` object.
3. The final confusing piece of background downloads is that you must tell the watchOS when the session has completed, so save the provided completion handler.

Of course, `sessionCompletion` doesn't yet exist, so add a final property to **SessionData**:

```
var sessionCompletion: (() -> Void)? = nil
```

You've simply created an optional delegate that takes no parameters and returns nothing. Now, what should you do with that property? That's right, call it from `downloadCompleted(for:data:)` in **SessionCache**, right after calling the other delegate method.

```
sessionData.sessionCompletion?()
sessionData.sessionCompletion = nil
```

Nothing to it, right? :]

At this point, after building and running the app, you'll start to see fresh tide data every hour on your complications.

Key Points

- Always use a data download, not a data task.
- Ensure you call both the session event's completion handler as well as the timeline provider's completion handler.

Chapter 10: Face Sharing

By Scott Grosch

While the ability to create and use **complications** has existed for years, being able to share the perfect watch face with your friends and customers is a newer feature. Most apps you develop will only have a single complication. Sometimes, however, you might provide multiple complications.

Consider the **TideWatch** app you built in previous chapters. When it makes sense to group multiple complications from your app *or other apps*, you can now offer a way for your customers to receive a preconfigured watch face easily.

> **Note**: You'll need a physical device to send a watch face from the iPhone to the Apple Watch.

Sharing Faces

There are four ways you can share a watch face:

1. Using the Watch app on your iOS device.
2. Directly from your watch.
3. Downloading a **watchface** file from the web.
4. Adding it via your custom iOS app.

From the iPhone

One of the simplest ways to share a watch face is by running the **Watch** app on your iPhone. When the app opens, you'll see all of the watch faces you have currently configured:

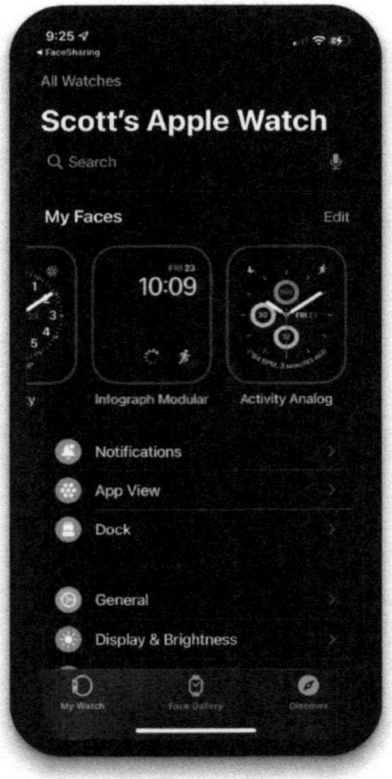

Long-press any of the watch faces. You'll see a sheet appear which will let you share the face:

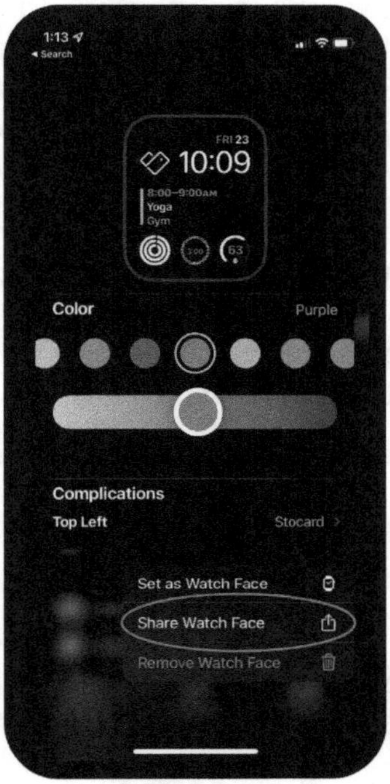

From the Apple Watch

It's even easier to share from the Apple Watch. From the home screen, long-press the watch face and choose the share icon. Then select to whom you'd like to send the watch face:

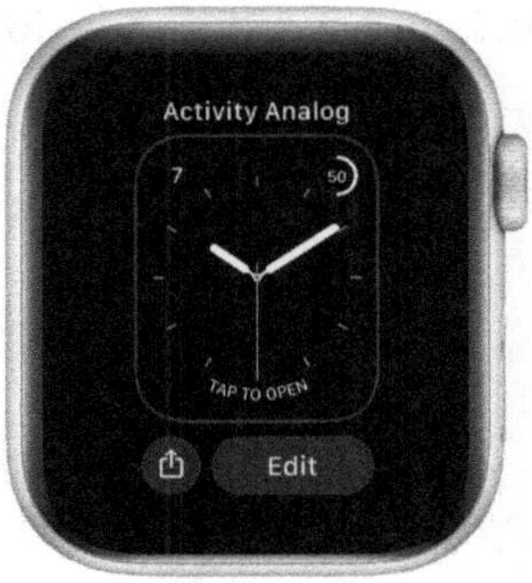

From the Web

If you want to share multiple watch faces, you may wish to host them on your app's website. Point your favorite browser to Apple's Human Interface Guide (HIG) (https://apple.co/3s33S5P). Scroll down to the **Technologies** section, and you'll see a download available for **Add Apple Watch Face**. Download the file, which is a DMG, and then double-click it. You'll see a window containing the developer license as well as an **Assets** folder.

The **Assets** folder contains multiple images you can place on your webpage to let customers know they can download a watch face. Each style of button contains images that work well with both light and dark mode websites. Apple has also provided the images in **PDF**, **PNG** and **SVG** formats.

Once you create a watch face on your physical device that looks the way you want with the appropriately placed complications, share the face with yourself by choosing the **Mail** app. Unlike the other sharing types, if you choose Mail, you'll get both the watch face file and a graphic showing how the face looks.

> **Note**: The preview is only included in the email if you share the face from the Watch app on the iPhone, not directly from the Apple Watch.

Now, you simply create a standard webpage that showcases your awesome watch face with a few simple steps:

1. Choose the **SVG** graphic you wish to use for the download button.
2. Save both files that you mailed to yourself when sharing the face.
3. Create a page that displays the watch face and has accompanying download buttons.

You can quickly create a page like this:

Using your favorite text editor, create a file called **index.html** somewhere on your Mac. It shouldn't be part of the Xcode project.

```
<html>
<head>
<link rel="stylesheet" href="style.css">
</head>
<body>
<h1>My Cool App</h1>
<p>We really think you'll love this watch face!</p>

<hr />
<div>
  <img src="preview.png">
  <br/>
  <br/>

  <a href="FaceToShare.watchface"
     type="application/vnd.apple.watchface">
    <img src="download.svg">
  </a>
</div>

<div>
  <p>
    You can scan the below QR code to install the watch face
from your
    paired iOS device.
  </p>
  <img alt="QR Code" class="qrcode" src="qrcode.png">
</div>
</body>
</html>
```

After saving the file, double-click on it in **Finder** to launch your web browser.

Obviously, that HTML shows how quickly you can make your watch faces available to your customers. A production website would, of course, look much nicer and include all appropriate HTML tags.

Notice, on the anchor tag, the <a> element, the referenced location is the watchface file. Then inside the anchor, the image points to the SVG graphic you chose from the HIG. That's one example of making a clickable "button" to download the watch face. Also, notice that the anchor tag's `type` attribute is `application/vnd.apple.watchface`.

While the download button is great, you can't assume that your customer has arrived on your website while browsing on their phone. If they're surfing the web on their laptop, and decide they want your watch face, then providing a QR code that points to the downloadable watch face makes their life easier. They just pull out their phone, point at the screen and download your watch face.

Take a look at Watchfacely (https://www.watchfacely.com) for great examples of webpages providing shared watch faces. Health management (https://bit.ly/3s1zWXY) is a specific example showing a shared health management face.

From the iOS App

You have one final option for providing a preconfigured watch face. You can embed the face right into your iOS app. The advantage of this approach is that the person using your app doesn't have to transition to a website. You simply provide them some mechanism to send the face directly to the paired Apple Watch via one of the HIG buttons you downloaded.

Open **FaceSharing.xcodeproj** from this chapter's starter materials. You'll notice the project already includes a few items for you:

- The **FaceToShare.watchface** file.
- The appropriate HIG button to share the face is in **Assets.xcassets**.
- The face's preview image is in **Assets.xcassets**.
- **Session** with the standard boilerplate.

> **Note**: Be sure you include any **.watchface** file you add to Xcode in the **FaceSharing** target membership. If you use Xcode to add the file, that's automatic. If you drag the file in from Finder, then it isn't.

Unlike other chapters in this book, there's no watchOS target. iOS handles sending a watch face and only requires an active and paired Apple Watch.

Setting Up the Session

In Chapter 4, "Watch Connectivity", you learned about `WCSession` and `WCSessionDelegate`. To know whether an Apple Watch is paired to the iOS device, you'll need the same type of session running. If there's not a paired Apple Watch, then you wouldn't want to provide the option to install a custom watch face.

Open **Session**. Add a property to `Session` to track whether or not you should show a share button, as well as the method which will update the value:

```
// 1
@MainActor
@Published
var showFaceSharing = false

private func updateFaceSharing(_ session: WCSession) {
  // 2
  let activated = session.activationState == .activated
  let paired = session.isPaired

  // 3
  Task { @MainActor in
    self.showFaceSharing = activated && paired
  }
}
```

In the preceding code:

1. You use `@Published` to notify SwiftUI when changes to the property occur. Since the property intends to determine if you should display a UI element, you'll also want to use `@MainActor` so that Xcode helps ensure you only update the property from the main thread.

2. Using the supplied `WCSession`, you determine whether the session is active on a paired Apple Watch. No need to check if the app is installed.

3. Finally, you set `showFaceSharing`, ensuring you first dispatch to the main queue since you're triggering UI updates.

Next, in `sessionDidBecomeInactive(_:)` and `session(_:activationDidCompleteWith:error:)`, you call the method you just wrote. So add this line to both methods:

```
updateFaceSharing(session)
```

Add one more delegate method:

```
func sessionWatchStateDidChange(_ session: WCSession) {
  updateFaceSharing(session)
}
```

This way, you've ensured `showFaceSharing` always knows whether or not there's an active and paired Apple Watch.

Showing the Share Button

Now open **ContentView**. Currently, you only show an image of the face which you'll send to the watch. You need to include a download button, but only if there's a paired Apple Watch.

Start by adding the following code, right after the `Image` line:

```
// 1
if session.showFaceSharing {
} else {
  // 2
  Text("Unable to share watch face")
    .font(.title)
  // 3
  Text("Please pair an Apple Watch first")
    .font(.title3)
}
```

Here's a code breakdown:

1. By looking at the published property you just configured in **Session**, SwiftUI can determine what to display.
2. If face sharing isn't available, you tell the user they can't share the face in a `.title` font.
3. It's also a good idea to identify *why* they can't share the face by telling them there's no paired Apple Watch in a slightly smaller `.title3` font.

Remember that SwiftUI reevaluates the `body` whenever a property marked as `@Published` changes. If face sharing *is* available, you need to call a method that transfers the face.

Add the following method:

```
// 1
func sendWatchFace() async {
  // 2
  guard let url = Bundle.main.url(
    forResource: "FaceToShare",
    withExtension: "watchface"
  ) else {
    // 3
    fatalError("You didn't include the watchface file in the
bundle.")
  }
}
```

Here's what's happening in that code:

1. You defined a method to transfer the face. Because it might take a bit of time, you mark the method as `async`.
2. You load the watchface file that you included in the iOS target.
3. While a `fatalError` call is usually bad, it's appropriate in this situation as you want to catch the missing bundle file during development rather than once you've published the app.

The library you'll use to actually perform the transfer comes from **ClockKit**. So, add the appropriate import to the top of the file:

```
import ClockKit
```

Finally, you'll use the `CLKWatchFaceLibrary` to perform the transfer. Add the following to the end of `sendWatchFace`:

```
// 1
let library = CLKWatchFaceLibrary()

// 2
do {
  // 3
  try await library.addWatchFace(at: url)
} catch {
  // 4
  print(error.localizedDescription)
}
```

In the preceding code:

1. As mentioned, you create an object of type `CLKWatchFaceLibrary`.
2. The transfer might fail, so you need to wrap the call in a `do/catch` block.
3. You `try` to perform `addWatchFace(at:)` by passing the URL of the face you loaded from the `Bundle`. As the method is asynchronous, you add the `await` keyword after `try`.
4. If the face can't be transferred, you'll need to handle the error. In a production app, that would likely mean displaying some type of alert.

> **Note**: Remember, it's always `try await`, never `await try`. You try to wait for the call to complete. You don't wait for a method to try and run.

According to Apple's documentation on `addWatchFace(at:)`:

> *All of the complications on the watch face must come from apps with a valid App Store ID, such as an app from the App Store or a TestFlight build. If you try to use complications from a development build, the system won't recognize the development ID as a valid App Store ID.*

Now it's time to use your new method. Go back to the `body` definition and inside of the `if` condition, add:

```
Button {
  Task { await sendWatchFace() }
} label: {
  Image("ShareButton")
}
```

That's pretty standard SwiftUI for adding a button with one exception. When the user clicks the button, you create a new top-level `Task`. The method `sendWatchFace` is asynchronous, but the button click's action isn't aware of the asynchronous method.

By wrapping the call in the `Task` block, you allow the method call to still properly run asynchronously. This is a common pattern you'll use when calling async methods from SwiftUI bodies.

At this point, you're ready to test things out. Build and run the app in the **Simulator**, not on your physical device. You'll see the message saying you can't share the watch face. The Simulator isn't configured with a paired watch face.

Build and run the app again, this time targeting your iPhone. This time you can share the watch face. Of course, you'll have to have a paired Apple Watch handy! :]

Tap the **add button**, and you'll be asked to add the face to your Apple Watch:

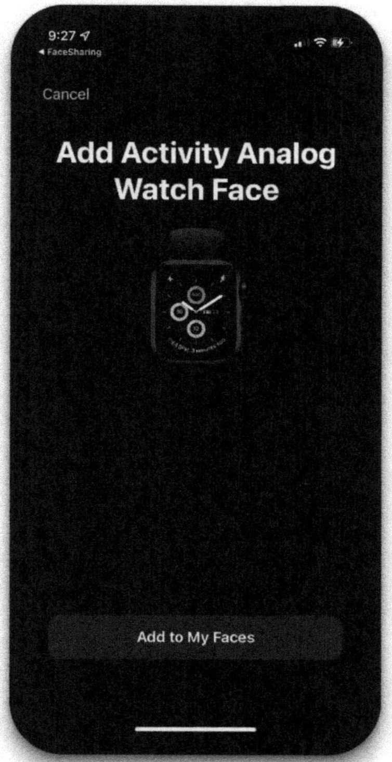

While it seems redundant since you just tapped the download button, Apple wants to make sure faces don't magically appear on your devices without you being aware.

> **Note**: Never install a face to the watch without the user explicitly requesting it via a download button.

After you tap **Add to My Faces**, go to the Watch app on your iPhone, and the new watch face should now be visible:

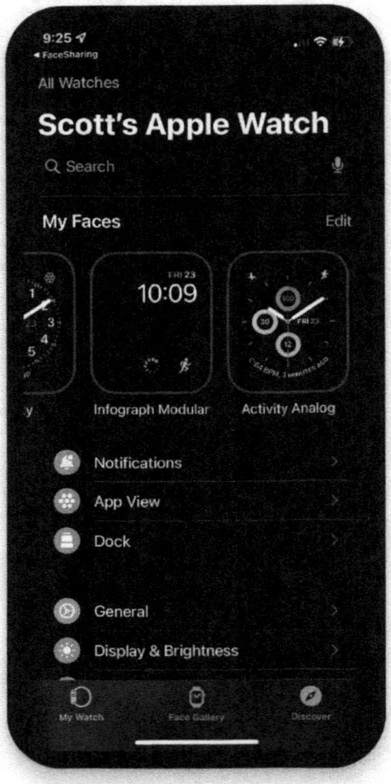

Finally, for the *pièce de résistance*. Set the newly installed watch face and then glance at your Apple Watch. You'll see your shiny new watch face!

Key Points

- Only install a watch face if the user requests it.
- Don't offer to install a watch face if there is no paired device.
- Anyone can create shareable watch faces, but only you can offer them from inside the app.

Where to Go From Here?

- The sample materials for this chapter contain a **web** folder that includes the full source to the sample webpage.
- Check out the amazing Watchfacely (https://www.watchfacely.com) site for great examples of sharing faces via the web.
- Many sites on the web will generate QR codes for free, such as QR Code Generator (https://www.qr-code-generator.com).

Chapter 11: Sign in With Apple

By Scott Grosch

Sign in with Apple, or **SIWA**, has been around for a few years. Your customers will greatly appreciate the simplicity of registration and authentication when using a device with a screen as small as the Apple Watch.

You should consider this a bonus chapter, as there's nothing Apple Watch-specific related to SIWA. If you're already familiar with how to implement SIWA, feel free to skip this chapter. Due to the extra importance of a streamlined experience on the Apple Watch, I felt it made sense to include this content in the book.

> **Note**: To fully implement SIWA, you'll need a paid Apple developer account to set up the required identifiers and profiles.
>
> This chapter only deals with the watchOS parts of SIWA. Embedded Sign in with Apple JS, web server and developer portal configurations are outside the scope of this book.

Some vendors won't implement SIWA due to the anonymization of email addresses. When a customer emails the vendor with a support ticket, it's harder to locate the customer's account. However, you should keep in mind that your *user's* experience is what you should prioritize, not yours.

To Authenticate or not

Build and run the **SignIn** app from this chapter's starter materials. You'll see a simple screen that lets you choose which of two views to display. Tap the top button, and you're taken to the part of the app which doesn't require authentication. However, tap the second button, and you're asked to authenticate:

Authenticate via Username and Password

The authentication screen you currently see is what most apps present: a simple username and password entry view.

Take a look at **Authenticating/PasswordView**. For the Apple Watch, it's especially important to specify the text content type:

```
TextField("User Name", text: $userName)
  .textContentType(.username)

SecureField("Password", text: $password)
  .textContentType(.password)
```

Specifying the content type gives watchOS clues about how to present and handle the data. A `.username` or `.password` field can be appropriately linked to the keychain, for example.

Next, notice `isButtonDisabled` computed property:

```
private var isButtonDisabled: Bool {
  userName.trimmingCharacters(in: .whitespaces).isEmpty ||
password.isEmpty
}
```

As well as its use on the button:

```
Button("Sign In", action: signInTapped)
  .disabled(isButtonDisabled)
```

There's no point in letting the user tap the **Sign In** button if they haven't properly supplied all required fields.

> **Note**: Instead of disabling the button, you could also present an alert sheet when the user provides invalid data.

Finally, notice how self-contained the view is. It performs a single task, which is to gather the input. When your user taps the Sign In button, *something* happens, but this view doesn't care what. It simply delegates the work elsewhere by passing the details to the `completionHandler`.

Handling Sign-in

Now switch to **Authenticating/SignInView**. The `SignInView` is where you handle the *how* of your app's login. The first piece you'll notice is the use of app storage:

```
@AppStorage("userName") private var storedUserName = ""
```

Tracking the username isn't a detail of `PasswordView` because it shouldn't care where the username comes from. While app storage will be a common location, you might just as easily store the user's information in Core Data.

The completion handler for the `PasswordView` performs your actual authentication:

```
private func userPasswordCompletion(userName: String, password:
String) {
  // 1
  storedUserName = userName

  // 2
  var request = URLRequest(
    url: URL(string: "https://your.site.com/login")!
  )
  request.httpMethod = "POST"
  // request.httpBody = ...

  DispatchQueue.main.async {
    // 3
    onSignedIn("some token here")

    // 4
    dismiss()
  }
}
```

Here, the code:

1. Updates the username you're storing with whatever value the user supplied. If they change usernames, they likely want to use the same one next time.
2. Generates your `URLRequest` as appropriate to send the username and password to your web service.
3. Once the authentication successfully returns, it calls the completion handler supplied to `SignInView`. The example above assumes your web service returns some type of token to use for future network calls.
4. Normally, this view is pushed onto a stack or displayed in a modal dialog. If authentication was successful, it dismisses the view.

Your app may send a `Decodable` object back, it might supply values in a header or any other combination of responses. You'll need to update the code as appropriate. Keep three key details in mind:

- Call the completion handler with the appropriate response data.
- Dismiss the view if authentication was successful.
- Ensure you're working against the main thread when calling your completion handler, dismissing the view and presenting any errors.

> **Note**: Don't mark the method as `@MainActor` as your don't want the network call running on the main thread.

Signing in With Apple

At this point, your login screen is fully functional. Functional, but not friendly. I don't know about you, but I always struggle to draw letters exactly as the Apple Watch wants them. Wouldn't it be better to have a Sign in with Apple button available?

Time to finally do some coding!

Adding the SIWA Button

While still editing **SignInView**, add an import to the top of the file:

```
import AuthenticationServices
```

`AuthenticationServices` provides the code necessary for SIWA.

Now add two stub methods to the `SignInView` in this file:

```
private func onRequest(request: ASAuthorizationAppleIDRequest) {
}

private func siwaCompletion(result: Result<ASAuthorization,
Error>) {
}
```

You'll populate both methods in a moment, but they're required for the button to be used inside `body`. Now place the following code between the `Text` and `PasswordView` elements in the `body`:

```
SignInWithAppleButton(onRequest: onRequest, onCompletion:
siwaCompletion)
  .signInWithAppleButtonStyle(.white)

Divider()
  .padding()
```

Take a look in the Canvas, inside of Xcode, and you'll now see your shiny new SIWA button:

That's all it takes to place the button. Now that SIWA has full SwiftUI support, you no longer need to implement a `UIViewRepresentable` yourself. Nice.

Configuring the Request

You'll configure the request in the `onRequest(request:)` stub you generated. Add the following code there:

```
request.requestedScopes = [.fullName]
request.state = "some state string"
```

You told Apple that you need to know the **full name** of the person who is authenticating. `requestedScopes` allows for an `.email` option as well, but you should *only* request it if you need it. Keep in mind that most users will hide their email from you and use Apple's relay service. Apple will provide you a unique identifier to represent the user in your database, so don't ask for the email just so you have a unique "key" to represent the user.

`state` returns to you unmodified in the credential Apple supplies. You can provide whatever user-defined state you wish as it's simply echoed back to you in Apple's response.

Optionally, you may use `nonce` to mitigate replay attacks. A replay attack occurs when a malicious user copies and resends a data packet to you. By using a unique `nonce` value in every request, you ensure that Apple sent the packet you received. At the top of `SignInView`, add a private property:

```
private let nonce = UUID().uuidString
```

Then, inside `onRequest(request:)` set the request's nonce:

```
request.nonce = nonce
```

Note: Decoding and validating the nonce is outside the scope of this chapter.

Handling the Reply

When you get a reply back from Apple, there are three possible outcomes:

1. The authentication failed.
2. This is the first time successfully authenticating against your app.
3. You successfully authenticated, and it's not the first time.

To handle the first case, add the following code to `siwaCompletion(result:)`:

```
guard
  // 1
  case .success(let authorization) = result,
  // 2
  let credential = authorization.credential as?
ASAuthorizationAppleIDCredential
else {
  // 3
  if case .failure(let error) = result {
    print("Failed to authenticate: \
(error.localizedDescription)")
  }

  return
}
```

In the preceding code:

1. First, you store the `authorization` returned from Apple on success.
2. Next, you retrieve the `ASAuthorizationAppleIDCredential`.
3. If either of the first two steps fails and an error returns, display it. Your production code should, of course, display a message to the user as opposed to just printing to the console.

If a failure didn't occur, then you handle either login or registration. If `fullName`, which you requested in `onRequest(request:)` via `requestedScopes`, contains a value, then this is the first time you've authenticated this user.

If `fullName` is `nil`, then you've authenticated an existing user. It's unfortunate, but Apple will only return the user's full name and email address the *first time*. It's your responsibility to save that data in an app-appropriate way.

In your method, you'll simply check the property's value. Add the following code after the `guard` block you just added:

```
if credential.fullName == nil {
  // You've logged in an existing user account.
} else {
  // The user does not exist, so register a new account.
}
```

Depending on your app's configuration, you'll then need to take appropriate action. Usually, that means making a call to your web server to generate a new account or sign in to an existing account. In either case, you'll likely want to pass the `credential.user`, `credential.identityToken` and `credential.authorizationCode` to your server.

Note: Remember to call `onSignedIn()` after contacting your web server.

There's a critical component of new user registration to keep in mind, which you'll address next.

Storing the User Credentials

As it was mentioned in the previous section, Apple will only provide the name and email address the *first time* you authenticate. In consequence, if the registration call you make to your web server fails for any reason, you have to have a way to try again. Consider a scenario where your web server crashes or the Apple Watch loses network connectivity when you try to register with your server.

You should use some form of secure storage to store the data you need for registration until your server successfully registers the user. You can use the KeyChain, Core Data or any other secure storage mechanism that doesn't require the network.

The `user` property of the `credential` contains the unique identifier that Apple assigned to your user. You'll likely want to pass that identifier to all the calls you send to your web server. A simple way to handle that requirement is to add another `@AppStorage` to the top of `SignInView`:

```
@AppStorage("userCredential") private var userCredential = ""
```

And then, at the end of `siwaCompletion(result:)`, assign the value:

```
userCredential = credential.user
```

Storing Their Name Properly

If you've requested the user's full name, keep in mind that the value provided is a `PersonNameComponents`, not a `String`. To display the name, use the appropriate formatter, like so:

```
PersonNameComponentsFormatter.localizedString(
  from: nameComponents,
  style: .default
)
```

Different cultures display names differently, so you should never assume it's safe to send something like this to your server:

```
let me = credential.fullName
let badNameExample = "\(me.givenName) \(me.familyName)"
```

You may be tempted to use the formatter and then send *that* value to the web server. Don't do that either! Users from one country may see names of users from another country, so you want to ensure each person sees the name formatted correctly for their locale.

`PersonNameComponents` is `Codable`, meaning it's incredibly simple to send to your web server:

```
let encoder = JSONEncoder()
guard let data = try? encoder.encode(credential.fullName) else {
  // handle error appropriately
  return
}

let encoded = data.base64EncodedString()
```

Send the `encoded` value to your web server for storage. When you retrieve the name from your web server, perform the operations in reverse:

```
let decoder = JSONDecoder()

guard
  let data = Data(base64Encoded: encoded),
  let components = try? decoder.decode(
    PersonNameComponents.self,
    from: data
  )
else {
  // handle error appropriately
  return
}

let name = PersonNameComponentsFormatter.localizedString(
  from: components,
  style: .short
)
```

Key Points

- Adding SIWA is relatively easy, so use it wherever possible.
- Ensure that you store new user registration details local to the device until your app's web server performs a successful registration.
- Request the user's name and email address only if you truly need them.
- Keep in mind that most email addresses you receive will be an Apple relay address.
- Always store the full `PersonNameComponents` details on your web server.

Where to Go From Here?

For full details on SIWA, please see Apple's document, *Sign in with Apple (*https://apple.co/3uWndWk*)*.

Vapor (https://vapor.codes) is a great server-side option when using Sign in with Apple. See our book, *Server-Side Swift with Vapor (*https://bit.ly/3pL3doK*)*, for complete implementation details.

Chapter 12: HealthKit

By Scott Grosch

Apple Watch is an incredible device for tracking health and fitness. The sheer number of apps related to workout tracking is staggering. Therefore, in this chapter, you'll build a workout tracking...

No! Why not do something a bit different? In **Chapter 7, "Lifecycle"**, you built an app to help kids know how long to brush their teeth. Did you know that Apple Health has a section for tracking that?

1. Open the Apple Health app *on your iPhone*.
2. Tap **Browse** in the toolbar.
3. Tap **Other Data** from the **Health Categories** list.
4. You'll see **Toothbrushing** in the **No Data Available** section.

Who knew? :] Might as well log the fact you brushed your teeth, right?

> **Note**: There's nothing different about using HealthKit on the Apple Watch. However, it's such a pervasive use case that I wanted to include a chapter on it.

> **Note**: While the simulator can read and write to Apple Health, you can't launch the Apple Health app yourself. You'll need a physical device to truly complete this chapter.

Adding HealthKit

The starter materials for this chapter contain a slightly modified version of the Toothbrush app you built previously. **HealthKit** is one of the frameworks that requires permission from the user before you use it since it contains personal information.

When using HealthKit you'll also need to enable a background mode to specify the type of session that watchOS should use.

Signing & Capabilities

After opening **Health.xcodeproj**, from the starter materials, you need to add the HealthKit capability to Xcode:

1. In the Project Navigator (**Command-1**) select the project.
2. Select the the **Health Watch App** target.
3. Select **Signing & Capabilities**.
4. Click **+ Capability**.

5. In the dialog that appears, choose **HealthKit.**
6. Click **+ Capability** again and this time choose **Background Modes**.
7. For the session type, select **Self Care**.

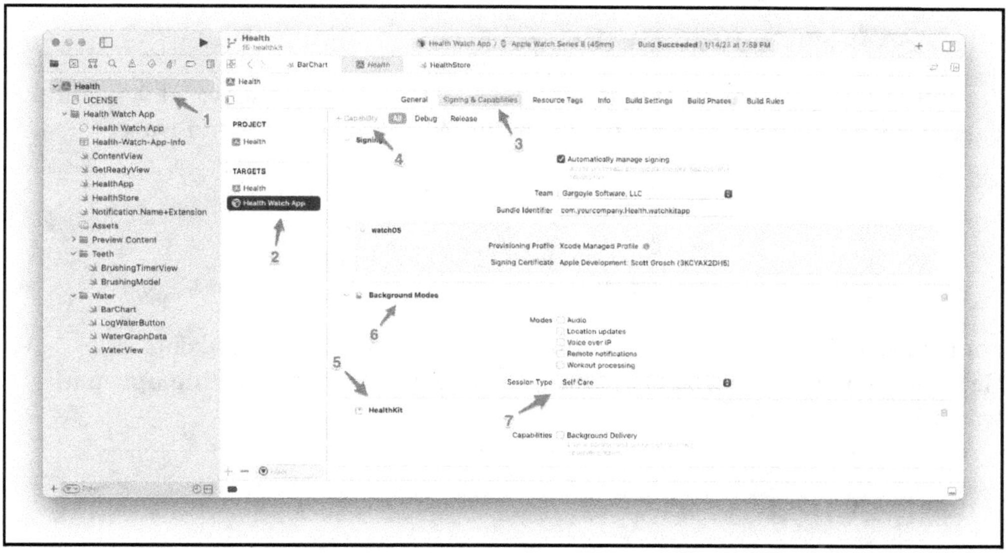

Note: Refer back to Chapter 7, “Lifecycle” for an explanation of the background modes.

Info.plist Descriptions

Once you've done that, click on the **Info** tab and add two keys related to privacy:

- Privacy - Health Share Usage Description
- Privacy - Health Update Usage Description

For the first key, set the value to the reason you're asking the user to let you write data to HealthKit. For example, you might put: **Tracks brushing and water consumption.**

> **Note**: Spoiler alert, you'll also add water tracking to the app.

For the second key, set the value to the reason why you need to read data from HealthKit. For example, you might put: **Bodyweight helps determine optimal water intake requirements.**

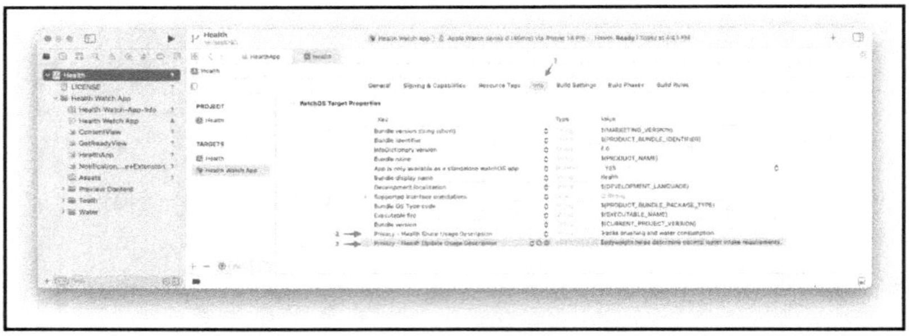

Creating the Store

Select the **Health Watch App** folder in the Project Navigator.Create a new swift file and name it **HealthStore**, using the following contents:

```
// 1
import Foundation
import HealthKit

final class HealthStore {
  // 2
  static let shared = HealthStore()

  // 3
  private var healthStore: HKHealthStore?
```

```
    // 4
    private init() {
      // 5
      guard HKHealthStore.isHealthDataAvailable() else {
        return
      }

      healthStore = HKHealthStore()
    }
  }
```

What's that code doing? Here's a breakdown:

1. HealthKit is a framework, so you need to import the package.
2. The `HealthStore` is a singleton.
3. You need a variable to hold the `HKHealthStore`.
4. A private initializer ensures that callers must use the `shared` singleton instance.
5. If the device can't use Apple Health, you quietly exit. If it can, you initialize the `HKHealthStore`.

Your wrapper class implements the singleton pattern because Apple specifies that you should only create a single instance of `HKHealthStore` for your app. If the device can't use HealthKit, then you shouldn't try to initialize the store.

To initialize `HealthStore`, add the following code to **HealthApp** just after the `NavigationView`'s closing curly bracket:

```
.task {
  _ = HealthStore.shared
}
```

`.task` runs a single time when the app starts. Even though you threw away the return of the call to `HealthStore.shared`, the initializer ran.

> **Note**: There are multiple camps of thought on a class like `HealthStore`. Some people like the singleton pattern, while others feel the class should be an `ObservableObject` so you can place it into the environment. In the case of `HealthStore`, I chose the singleton pattern so it would be available outside of a SwiftUI `View`, if necessary.

Now that you have HealthKit configured, it's time to track some data.

Tracking Brushing

Apple Health stores activities differently depending on the type of data. For example, when brushing your teeth, the Apple Health app tracks the start and end times.

Brushing HealthKit Configuration

Add the following property to your `HealthStore` class so that Apple Health knows you're going to log data related to brushing your teeth:

```
private let brushingCategoryType =
HKCategoryType(.toothbrushingEvent)
```

Now it's time to ask the user for permission to read and write data related to how often they brush their teeth. Add the following code to the end of the initializer:

```
Task {
  try await healthStore!.requestAuthorization(
    toShare: [brushingCategoryType],
    read: [brushingCategoryType]
  )
}
```

When your app calls `requestAuthorization(toShare:read:)`, the user will see a request to authorize your app to read and write the specified data. As long as you don't ask for types that you haven't previously, watchOS will only display the request a single time.

Wrapping the asynchronous call in a `Task` lets you use the call in a method not marked `async`.

Sharp-eyed readers will notice that `requestAuthorization(toShare:read:)` is a throwing method, yet you've not protected against the method throwing. A peculiar side effect of `Task` is that *it eats all exceptions*.

Build and run. Once it launches, watchOS will present screens to you requesting permission to read and write to Apple Health. Once you've approved both read and write access, relaunch the app. This time, there's no prompt as the call to `requestAuthorization(toShare:read:)` doesn't include any new types.

Now you'll add a method to log when you've brushed your teeth. Add this code to `HealthStore`:

```
// 1
func logBrushing(startDate: Date) async throws {
  // 2
  guard
    let healthStore,
    healthStore.authorizationStatus(for: brushingCategoryType)
== .sharingAuthorized
  else {
    return
  }

  // 3
  let sample = HKCategorySample(
    type: brushingCategoryType,
    value: HKCategoryValue.notApplicable.rawValue,
    start: startDate,
    end: Date.now
  )

  // 4
  try await healthStore.save(sample)
}
```

Here's what's happening:

1. You define a method that takes the `Date` when the user started brushing their teeth and note that it's both asynchronous and can throw.

2. At any point, your user can enable or disable access to Apple Health. Therefore, you need a way to know whether they're letting you write data for brushing their teeth.

3. You create a sample, which is what HealthKit stores, of type `brushingCategoryType`. Brushing doesn't have a *value*, so you pass the `HKCategoryValue.notApplicable.rawValue` enum value. Then you log the start and end time of the brushing.

4. Finally, you save the sample to HealthKit.

Note: You can't check for read access, only write. If you don't have read access, you just get no results back.

Based on your app's configuration, you need to decide whether to silently `return` in the `guard` clause of step two or throw some type of exception. In this app, it makes sense to let them brush their teeth and get the 30-second timer without writing to Apple Health.

All that's left is to update the session end to call `logBrushing(startDate:)`.

Open **BrushingModel** inside the **Teeth** folder. You'll recognize this file from Chapter 7: "Lifecycle". Near the bottom of `extendedRuntimeSessionDidStart(_:)`, you'll find the line of code that invalidates the session:

```
self.session.invalidate()
```

When the session completes successfully, you need to write to Apple Health. Replace that line of code with:

```
// 1
Task {
  // 2
  try? await HealthStore.shared.logBrushing(startDate:
self.started)

  // 3
  self.session.invalidate()
}
```

The pattern is probably starting to look familiar:

1. You're in a method that is *not* `async`, but you want to call an `async` method, so you pass the call to a `Task`.
2. Log the fact that the user finished brushing their teeth. If it fails, you probably want to ignore it as there's nothing for the user to do.
3. Mark the session as complete once the update to Apple Health finishes.

It's time to build and run. Before doing so, you may wish to change the value of `secondsPerRound` in **Teeth/BrushingModel** to something smaller, like 2.0, so that you don't have to wait two minutes to see results.

Once you've built and run the app, tap the brush button and watch the magic happen. When the timer runs out, switch over to the Apple Health app. Now repeat the steps from the start of this chapter to look at the toothbrushing category, and you'll see an entry:

Tracking Water

Like brushing their teeth, many kids have a hard time remembering to drink water. Seems like a great addition to your app!

While brushing teeth logged time rather than a value, water intake is the opposite. You're likely less concerned with *when* they drank water and more interested in *how much* water they drank each day.

There's quite a bit of work to do to support water intake. This may be a good time to take a quick break and grab a snack!

Updating Permissions

Recommended water intake is based on body mass. So, you'll have to ask for two more types of data from HealthKit. In **HealthStore**, add:

```
private let waterQuantityType = HKQuantityType(.dietaryWater)
private let bodyMassType = HKQuantityType(.bodyMass)
```

Notice that you're now using quantity types, not category types.

Next, update the call to `requestAuthorization(toShare:read:)` so that it includes the new identifiers:

```
Task {
  try await healthStore!.requestAuthorization(
    toShare: [brushingCategoryType, waterQuantityType],
    read: [brushingCategoryType, waterQuantityType,
bodyMassType]
  )
}
```

Pay attention to the fact that you would like to read the person's weight, or body mass, but you have no reason to write their weight. **Don't request permissions that you don't need**.

Build and run now, and you'll notice that Apple Health again asks for permissions. The dialog appeared again because you added new items to the list of authorizations you're requesting. You'll also notice that nothing related to brushing teeth is shown in the request, as you've already answered those questions. Don't give permission quite yet, just stop the app in Xcode. You will handle the permission change in a little bit.

Water HealthKit Configuration

Time to update the `HealthStore` to handle water. Add the following to **HealthStore**:

```
// 1
var isWaterEnabled: Bool {
  let status = healthStore?.authorizationStatus(
    for: waterQuantityType
  )

  return status == .sharingAuthorized
}

// 2
func logWater(quantity: HKQuantity) async throws {
  guard isWaterEnabled else {
    return
  }

  // 3
  let sample = HKQuantitySample(
    type: waterQuantityType,
    quantity: quantity,
    start: Date.now,
    end: Date.now
  )

  // 4
  try await healthStore!.save(sample)
}
```

In the preceding code, you:

1. Need to know whether the user is *currently* allowing you to write water-related data.
2. Implement an `async` method to store water consumption as you did for brushing your teeth.
3. Generate a sample to save. Notice how you specify an actual *quantity* this time, and the start and end dates are the current time.
4. Save the data, if you can. It's safe to force unwrap the `healthStore` as your status check succeeded.

Log Water Button

To keep the app simple, you'll provide two buttons to let the user enter an amount of water. Inside the **Water** folder, you'll find a file named **LogWaterButton**. I've cheated a bit in the interest of simplicity and hardcoded two water sizes based on whether you're using the metric system. A real app should handle all measurement systems, not just assume metric or US.

When the user taps the button, you need to generate the appropriately sized `HKQuantity` to tell Apple Health how much water the person drank. Edit `tapped()` and paste:

```
// 1
let unit: HKUnit
let value: Double

if Locale.current.measurementSystem == .metric {
  // 2
  unit = .literUnit(with: .milli)
  value = size == .small ? 250 : 500
} else {
  // 3
  unit = .fluidOunceUS()
  value = size == .small ? 8 : 16
}

// 4
let quantity = HKQuantity(unit: unit, doubleValue: value)

// 5
onTap(quantity)
```

Here's what the code is doing:

1. HealthKit uses an `HKUnit` to identify the unit type for the value you'll store.
2. If the user's device uses the metric system, you create a value in milliliters.
3. If the user's device isn't using metric, they're clearly from the United States and thus want fluid ounces. Yes, that's sarcasm. I told you we were cheating here.
4. Using `unit` and `value`, you create an `HKQuantity`, which you can later convert to an `HKSample` for saving.
5. You pass that quantity to the completion handler.

Water View

Now create another SwiftUI view called **WaterView** to act as the UI when taking a drink. Be sure to import HealthKit at the top of the file:

```
import HealthKit
```

In the body, replace the default "Hello, World!" text with the following code. Don't worry about the closure argument list errors you see – you'll fix it in a moment:

```
// 1
ScrollView {
  VStack {
    // 2
    if HealthStore.shared.isWaterEnabled {
      Text("Add water")
        .font(.headline)

      HStack {
        LogWaterButton(size: .small) {  }
        LogWaterButton(size: .large) {  }
      }
      .padding(.bottom)
    } else {
      // 3
      Text("Please enable water tracking in Apple Health.")
    }
  }
}
```

The view right now is pretty simple:

1. You have a vertically scrolling view to contain everything. You don't need the `ScrollView` right now, but you will soon.
2. If the user lets you write to Apple Health, display some text and the two buttons to add the amounts of water consumed.
3. If they don't grant permissions, display a message.

While you shouldn't even present this view to the user if they haven't granted write access, it's always a good idea to protect as many areas of the app as possible. You may refactor other views and inadvertently remove a critical permission check.

When the user taps a button, you need to take action. So, implement:

```
private func logWater(quantity: HKQuantity) {
  Task {
    try await HealthStore.shared.logWater(quantity: quantity)
  }
}
```

The helper wraps the asynchronous call in `Task` since the SwiftUI button doesn't know how to call an `async`. In a production app, you'll likely want to set a `@State` that would result in the user seeing an alert on failure. Now that you have the helper method, call it on button taps:

```
LogWaterButton(size: .small) { logWater(quantity: $0) }
LogWaterButton(size: .large) { logWater(quantity: $0) }
```

Updating ContentView

In **ContentView**, import HealthKit at the top of the file:

```
import HealthKit
```

Create another state property:

```
@State private var wantsToDrink = false
```

And then, right after the existing `Button`, add another one:

```
if HealthStore.shared.isWaterEnabled {
  Button {
    wantsToDrink.toggle()
  } label: {
    Image(systemName: "drop.fill")
      .foregroundColor(.blue)
  }
}
```

If, and only if, the user allows your app to write water consumption to Apple Health, you'll show a button that toggles the state variable.

Right after the `.sheet` which displays `BrushingTimerView()`, add one to display the `WaterView()`:

```
.sheet(isPresented: $wantsToDrink) {
  WaterView()
}
```

Build and run. HealthKit will ask you for permission to read and write water consumption data. Once you approve, the dialog goes away and... nothing looks different!

Where's your water button? Take a moment to think through what's happening to see if you can figure it out.

Getting the View to Update

Remember that in SwiftUI, the body only updates if something being observed, like a `@State` property, changes. SwiftUI doesn't know when the value for `HealthStore.shared.isWaterEnabled` changes. You need to explicitly tell the view that a change has happened.

Start by adding another `let` in **Notification.Name+Extension**:

```
static let healthStoreLoaded = Notification.Name(rawValue:
UUID().uuidString)
```

Then, in **HealthStore**, at the end of the `Task` in the initializer, post that notification:

```
await MainActor.run {
  NotificationCenter.default.post(name: .healthStoreLoaded,
object: nil)
}
```

Once HealthKit finishes asking for any required permissions, you let the rest of the app know via the notification. Remember that you're no longer on the main thread because you're running inside of a `Task` from a static initializer. Since you intend for the notification you're posting to trigger a UI update, you dispatch the post to the `MainActor`, which means the thread running the UI.

Change back to **ContentView** and add two new properties:

```
// 1
@State private var waitingForHealthKit = true

// 2
private let healthStoreLoaded =
NotificationCenter.default.publisher(
  for: .healthStoreLoaded
)
```

Here's what those properties are for:

1. Using a `@State` variable to track whether HealthKit has completed checking permissions means the body will see the update.
2. A publisher is the SwiftUI way of identifying a notification that you'll listen for.

Next, wrap the code inside the body's `VStack` with a check:

```
if waitingForHealthKit {
  Text("Waiting for HealthKit prompt.")
} else {
  // Existing code from VStack
}
```

Having the body look at `@State` means the view will refresh when it changes.

Finally, right after the existing `.onReceive(stopBrusing)`, add one more:

```
.onReceive(healthStoreLoaded) { _ in
  self.waitingForHealthKit = false
}
```

Once the notification is received, you update the property, which causes the view to refresh. To force HealthKit to ask for permissions the next time you run the app, delete the app from the watch. If you are running on the simulator, you can also reset the simulator by going to its menu and selecting
Device ▸ Erase All Content and Settings....

Build and run, this time tapping the water icon and then one of the two buttons. Once you've done so, switch to the Apple Health app on your iPhone and check out the water category in the **Nutrition** section. Congratulations, you drank some water! :]

Writing the data is great, but what about viewing it? You need to present the data to your users, especially on the Apple Watch, where the Apple Health app is mysteriously missing.

Reading Single Day Data

Common practice bases the amount of water you should drink on how much you weigh. It would be great to tell the user how much water they still need to drink today.

Querying HealthKit

In **HealthStore**, add a method to determine the user's current body mass:

```
// 1
private func currentBodyMass() async throws -> Double? {
  // 2
  guard let healthStore else {
    throw HKError(.errorHealthDataUnavailable)
  }

  // 3
  let descriptor = HKSampleQueryDescriptor(
    predicates: [.quantitySample(type: bodyMassType)],
    sortDescriptors: [SortDescriptor(\.startDate,
order: .reverse)],
    limit: 1
  )

  // 4
  let results = try await descriptor.result(for: healthStore)
  return results.first?.quantity.doubleValue(for: .pound())
}
```

Here's a breakdown:

1. You create an `async` wrapper to get the user's body mass.
2. If the store isn't assigned, then you throw an error.
3. You only want the current weight, so you sort the results by the start date in descending order, and limit to just a single result.
4. Read the results from the query and return the first item, converted to pounds. If there's no value, then a `nil` will be returned.

Hardcoding pounds here seems wrong, doesn't it? What about kilograms or stones? In the United States, the general theory is you divide your body weight in half and then drink that many ounces of water a day. Countries using the metric system would multiply their weight in kilograms by 0.033 to accomplish the same thing.

Coding every type of calculation would be a difficult task. Instead, take advantage of Apple providing the tools you need to convert between different measurements for you. By *internally* using pounds and ounces, you can perform a single known calculation and then display it to the user in their preferred measurement system.

Now that you potentially know how much they weigh, it's time to determine how much they've already drank today. In **HealthStore**, add:

```
private func drankToday() async throws -> (
  ounces: Double,
  amount: Measurement<UnitVolume>
) {
  guard let healthStore else {
    throw HKError(.errorHealthDataUnavailable)
  }

  // 1
  let dateRangePredicate = HKQuery.predicateForSamples(
    withStart: Calendar.current.startOfDay(for: Date.now),
    end: Date.now,
    options: .strictStartDate
  )

  // 2
  let sumPredicate = HKSamplePredicate.quantitySample(
    type: waterQuantityType,
    predicate: dateRangePredicate
  )

  // 3
  let descriptor = HKStatisticsQueryDescriptor(predicate:
sumPredicate, options: .cumulativeSum)

  // 4
  guard let quantity = try await descriptor.result(for:
healthStore)?.sumQuantity() else {
    return (ounces: 0, amount: .init(value: 0, unit: .liters))
  }

  // 5
  let ounces = quantity.doubleValue(for: .fluidOunceUS())
  let liters = quantity.doubleValue(for: .liter())

  // 6
  return (ounces, .init(value: liters, unit: .liters))
```

```
}
```

That method is a bit more complicated:

1. You want to determine all water consumed between the start of the day and now.
2. Tell HealthKit that the predicate relates to water samples.
3. Using an `HKStatisticsQueryDescriptor` lets you ask HealthKit to add all the values via the `.cumulativeSum`, so you get a single result.
4. If you don't have read permission or data, you state that the user drank 0 liters.
5. return both the number of US fluid ounces and the number of liters the user drank.

You provide the numerical value of ounces so you can perform math on it later. Using `Measurement<UnitVolume>` makes it easier for consumers to display the data in whatever format they need. Liters tend to be the "standard" value to use by default.

Finally, write the public method to determine what to display to the user:

```
func currentWaterStatus() async throws -> (
  Measurement<UnitVolume>, Double?
) {
  // 1
  let (ounces, measurement) = try await drankToday()

  // 2
  guard let mass = try? await currentBodyMass() else {
    return (measurement, nil)
  }

  // 3
  let goal = mass / 2.0
  let percentComplete = ounces / goal

  // 4
  return (measurement, percentComplete)
}
```

In the preceding code, you:

1. First, determine how much water the person drank today.
2. If you can't determine how much they weigh, you send back the water measurement with no percentage.
3. Then, perform simple math to determine how far they are towards the daily goal.
4. Return the water measurement and the percentage complete.

Notice that a single calculation is performed internally against US conversions, but what goes outside to the user is a `Measurement<UnitVolume>` using appropriate types.

Updating WaterView

Add two properties to **WaterView**:

```
@State private var consumed = ""
@State private var percent = ""
```

Then write the method which will populate those properties:

```
// 1
@MainActor
private func updateStatus() async {
  // 2
  guard
    let (measurement, percent)
      = try? await HealthStore.shared.currentWaterStatus()
  else {
    consumed = "0"
    percent = "Unknown"
    return
  }

  // 3
  consumed = consumedFormat.string(from: measurement)

  // 4
  self.percent = percent?
    .formatted(.percent.precision(.fractionLength(0))) ??
"Unknown"
}
```

Apologies for the formatting required to keep the lines from wrapping. Here's what's happening:

1. This method will be called from other threads, so make sure watchOS always runs the update on the main thread.
2. If you can't read the current water status, you set a couple of default values.
3. If you can read the data, you format the amount of water consumed via a `MeasurementFormatter` that you'll create in a moment.
4. Taking advantage of Foundation's new number formatters, you either calculate the daily percentage consumed or specify that it's`"Unknown"` if you couldn't determine the person's weight.

To resolve the compiler error, add the following formatter at the bottom of the file, outside of the `struct`:

```
private let consumedFormat: MeasurementFormatter = {
  var fmt = MeasurementFormatter()
  fmt.unitOptions = .naturalScale
  return fmt
}()
```

Next, update the `body` to show the data by adding this code right after the existing `HStack`:

```
HStack {
  Text("Today:")
    .font(.headline)
  Text(consumed)
    .font(.body)
}

HStack {
  Text("Goal:")
    .font(.headline)
  Text(percent)
    .font(.body)
}
```

Finally, update the status when the view appears by adding a `task` after the `ScrollView`:

```
.task {
  await updateStatus()
}
```

To update the display if you record new data, add the update line just before the end of the `Task` block in `WaterView`'s `logWater(quantity:)` method:

```
await updateStatus()
```

Build and run again. This time you'll see that you have logged water previously:

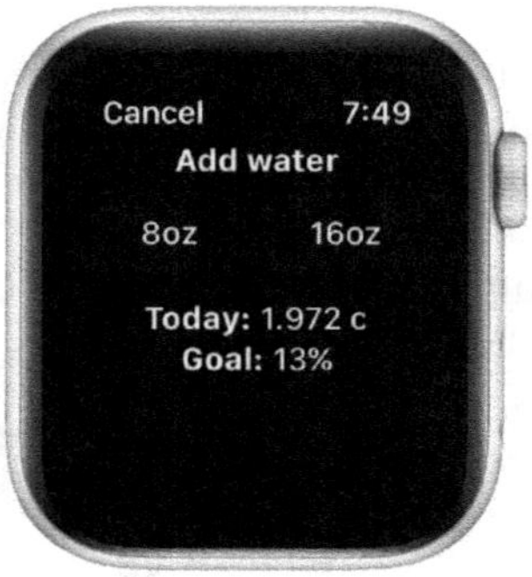

Reading Multiple Days of Data

Finally, to make the interface a bit nicer, why not show the amount of water the user consumed over the last week? Reading multiple days of data is a bit more complicated than reading just a single day. Back in **HealthStore**, add a new property to the top of the class:

```
private var preferredWaterUnit = HKUnit.fluidOunceUS()
```

And then set the value in the initializer, just before the `await MainActor.run` call:

```
if
  let types = try? await healthStore!.preferredUnits(for:
[waterQuantityType]),
  let type = types[waterQuantityType]
{
  preferredWaterUnit = type
}
```

As you can see, it's possible to determine what type of units your user prefers to see their measurements. You initialized the property to `HKUnit.fluidOuncesUS()` because there must be a value before the initializer ends.

Now add a new method to query the week's water consumption:

```
func waterConsumptionGraphData(
  completion: @escaping ([WaterGraphData]?) -> Void
) throws {
  guard let healthStore else {
    throw HKError(.errorHealthDataUnavailable)
  }

  // 1
  var start = Calendar.current.date(byAdding: .day, value: -6,
to: Date.now)!
  start = Calendar.current.startOfDay(for: start)

  let predicate = HKQuery.predicateForSamples(
    withStart: start,
    end: nil,
    options: .strictStartDate
  )

  // 2
  let query = HKStatisticsCollectionQuery(
    quantityType: waterQuantityType,
    quantitySamplePredicate: predicate,
    options: .cumulativeSum,
    anchorDate: start,
    intervalComponents: .init(day: 1)
  )

  // 3
  query.initialResultsHandler = { _, results, _ in
  }

  // 4
  query.statisticsUpdateHandler = { _, _, results, _ in
  }

  healthStore.execute(query)
}
```

Here's a code breakdown:

1. After verifying you can use HealthKit, you determine the start of the day six days ago and then set up a predicate to query all data from that time forward.
2. Then, you construct a query for water consumption, using the `predicate`, and ask HealthKit to sum up each day for you. You specify that it should perform the summation across day boundaries.
3. watchOS calls `initialResultsHandler` the first time the query completes.
4. watchOS calls `statisticsUpdateHandler` any time the user adds new data. By not specifying an end date on the predicate, you ensure that updates are captured.

Since both of the handlers perform the same actions, create a helper method that they'll both call:

```
private func updateGraph(
  start: Date,
  results: HKStatisticsCollection?,
  completion: @escaping ([WaterGraphData]?) -> Void
) {
  // 1
  guard let results else {
    return
  }

  var statistics: [WaterGraphData] = []

  // 2
  results.enumerateStatistics(from: start, to: Date.now)
{ statistic, _ in
    var value = 0.0

    if let sum = statistic.sumQuantity() {
      value = sum
        .doubleValue(for: self.preferredWaterUnit)
        .rounded(.up)
    }

    statistics.append(.init(value, for: statistic.startDate))
  }

  // 3
  completion(statistics)
}
```

Can you see why you don't want to duplicate that code twice? Here's what the code does:

1. If no results return, then you exit early.
2. Loop through each day, adding the total quantity of water, rounded up to the nearest whole number.
3. Pass the data back to the completion handler

Finally, call this method from the handlers:

```
query.initialResultsHandler = { _, results, _ in
  self.updateGraph(start: start, results: results, completion:
completion)
}

query.statisticsUpdateHandler = { _, _, results, _ in
  self.updateGraph(start: start, results: results, completion:
completion)
}
```

Back in **WaterView**, add a new property:

```
@State private var graphData: [WaterGraphData]?
```

Add the `BarChart` to the `body` just after the final `HStack`:

```
BarChart(data: graphData)
  .padding()
```

Then call the query method from the `.task` at the end of the `body`:

```
.task {
  await updateStatus()
  try? HealthStore.shared.waterConsumptionGraphData() {
    self.graphData = $0
  }
}
```

Build and run one last time. You have a nice bar chart that keeps itself updated as you record entries:

Key Points

- Make sure you don't try to track a type of data that isn't available on the OS versions you support. If you find yourself in that situation, ensure that you define the identifiers as optionals.
- Always use the user's preferred types when displaying or converting data. Never hardcode a unit type to display to the user.

13 Conclusion

As you've seen, the Apple Watch is a small device with endless possibilities if you know how to make the most of its potential.We hope this book has given you all the knowledge you need to create amazing apps using SwiftUI on your Apple Watch.

Remember that you can always go back to the chapters to review some specific concepts. We've tried to make it useful not only for beginners starting to develop for this device but also for more advanced programmers to have it as a reference book.

No matter what your case is, we hope you've really enjoyed this book. Remember, the best thing you can do from now on is try to implement everything you've learned. When you develop a new application, update an existing one or create one just for fun, don't forget that you can add great value to it if you accompany it with an Apple Watch app.

If you have any questions or comments as you work through this book, please stop by our forums at https://forums.kodeco.com and look for the particular forum category for this book.

Thank you again for purchasing this book. Your continued support makes the books, tutorials, videos and other things we do at Kodeco possible. We truly appreciate it!

– The *watchOS With SwiftUI by Tutorials* team

www.ingramcontent.com/pod-product-compliance
Lightning Source LLC
LaVergne TN
LVHW080045210926
848481LV00011B/3282
* 9 7 8 1 9 5 0 3 2 5 8 4 9 *